'Though God hath raised me high, yet this I count the glory of my crown; that I have reigned with your loves'

ELIZABETHAN ENGLAND

PETER BRIMACOMBE

Publication in this form copyright © Jarrold Publishing 2006.

Text copyright © Jarrold Publishing.

The moral right of the author has been asserted.

Series editor Angela Royston.

Designed by Simon Borrough.

Picture research by Sarah Hopper.

The publishers wish to thank thank Susan Doran, Lecturer in Early Modern History at Christ Church, Oxford, for reading the text.

The photographs are reproduced by kind permission of: Alamy 90b (Andrew Holt), 29 silhouette (Angelo Hornak), 46 (Lebrecht Music and Arts Photo Library), 42 (The National Trust Photo Library), 80 (Antony Nettle), 47t (Oxford Picture Library), 37b (Photofusion Picture Library), 72b (Brian Seed), 10b (Robert Steinforth); Art Archive 60t, 61b (British Museum/ Harper Collins Publishers); Berkeley Castle 73t; Bridgeman Art Library 10-11t (Ashmolean Museum, University of Oxford), 76, 85 (Beauchamp Collection, UK), 13b (Trustees of the Bedford Estate, Woburn Abbey), 26b (The Berger Collection at the Denver Art Museum, USA), 14b, 32t (Burghley House Collection, Lincolnshire), fc right (British Museum), 79t (Corsham Court, Wiltshire), 94b (Glasgow University Library, Scotland), 44 (Helmingham Hall Suffolk/ Mark Fiennes), 16b, 18 (Lambeth Palace Library, London), 66b (Timothy Millet Collection), 20 (Musée Condé, Chantilly, France), 40b (National Portrait Gallery of Ireland, Dublin), ifc–ifc flap, 12b, 25t, 39r, 48b, 64–65t, 71t, 75r, 82l, 84b (Private Collection), 25b, 61t, 84t, 87t (The Stapleton Collection), 87b (Traquair House, Innerleithen, Scotland), 27t, 33b and front flap (Victoria and Albert Museum, London), 58t (Yale Center for British Art/Paul Mellon Collection); Peter Brimacombe 22, 23t, 24b, 27b, 28, 30, 50t, 68t, 87c; British Library, London 19t, 23b, 49t, 59, 63c, 86, 92t; The Burton Constable Foundation 6b; Christie's Images Limited 45b, 81t; Corbis 64l, 72t, 73b (all Bettman), 88b (Gillian Darley/ Edifice), 70 (Richard Klune), 56 (Joel W. Rogers), 4 (WildCountry), 43r (Adam Woolfit); By Permission of the Trustees of Dulwich Picture Gallery 48t; By permission of the Folger Shakespeare Library 26l, 34b, 39l, 53t, 82r; Getty Images 68-69b; Jarrold Publishing (Unichrome) 8; Marquess of Salisbury/ Hatfield House 21l; Mary Evans Picture Library 32r, 37t, 54b, 55l, 65b; The Master and Fellows of Corpus Christi College, Cambridge 75l; The Master and Fellows of Trinity College, Cambridge 9l; National Maritime Museum, London fc left, 60b, 63, 67; National Portrait Gallery, London 5, 9r, 12l, 19r, 21r, 51r, 68b, 71b, 74, 88t, 90t, 91; NTPL 31, 38 (Derek Croucher), 17l, 93 (John Hammond), 29t (Angelo Hornak), 49b (Rob Judges), 43l (Geoff Morgan), 83 (Derrick E.Witty), 62t (George Wright); Photo RMN/© Droits réservés 11r; Collections of Plymouth City Museum and Art Gallery 6t, 41, 47b, 57l, 58b, 62b, 66t, 78; The Royal Collection © 2005, Her Majesty Queen Elizabeth II 10c, 16t, 17r; RSC/John Haynes 52t; The Shakespeare Birthplace Trust 33t, 50b; Shakespeare's Globe/John Tramper 55r; Tate, London 2005 34t, 35, 57r; TNA (PRO) SP12 215 79b; Topfoto 53b (HIP/ARPL), 7, 51l (HIP/British Library), 94t (HIP/British Museum), 24t (HIP/National Archives); V&A Images/Victoria and Albert Museum 1, 40t, 45t, 54t, 92b, bc; By kind permission of Viscount De L'Isle from his private collection 15, 36; Reproduced by the Trustees of the Wallace Collection, London 14t; Courtesy of Wilton House 52b.

The family trees were produced by Simon Borrough.

A CIP catalogue for this book is available from the British Library.

Published by:
Jarrold Publishing
Healey House, Dene Road, Andover,
Hampshire, SP10 2AA
www.britguides.com

Set in Minion.
Printed in Singapore.

ISBN-10: 1 84165 167 2
ISBN-13: 978 1 84165 167 5   1/06

 Pitkin is an imprint of Jarrold Publishing, Norwich.

CONTENTS

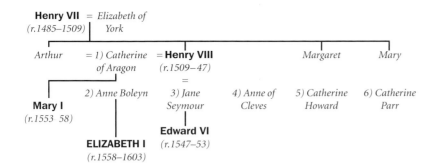

Henry VII (r.1485–1509)	= Elizabeth of York				
Arthur	= 1) Catherine of Aragon	= **Henry VIII** (r.1509–47)		Margaret	Mary
	2) Anne Boleyn	= 3) Jane Seymour	4) Anne of Cleves	5) Catherine Howard	6) Catherine Parr
Mary I (r.1553 58)					
	ELIZABETH I (r.1558–1603)	**Edward VI** (r.1547–53)			

THE TUDOR DYNASTY

The House of Tudor descending from Henry VII through his son Henry VIII with his six wives and three children, each of whom in turn inherited the English throne.

THE ELIZABETHAN ERA is amongst the most exciting and fascinating of any period of English history. A glamorous queen ruled a vibrant nation full of legendary figures such as Robert Dudley, Francis Drake, Walter Raleigh and the Earl of Essex – all of them international celebrities at the time. Great events unfolded with triumphs, such as the defeat of the Spanish Armada, and tragedies, like the long-term imprisonment and subsequent execution of Mary Queen of Scots. There were passionate love affairs, heroes and villains, glorious victories and heroic defeats, wily politicians, intrigue at the royal Court and sinister plotting everywhere. Elizabeth's reign was a long-running drama and it seems appropriate that William Shakespeare was writing at the time: the characters and events of his plays often mirrored Elizabethan life, and appeared to be interchangeable with it. Elizabeth presided over a glittering Court; she held centre stage as the drama queen – the star of the story.

✦

Shakespeare was one of the most successful Elizabethans, as popular today as in his lifetime, creating not only a series of brilliant plays and sonnets, but enriching and extending the English language by inventing words such as 'watchdog', 'hot-blooded' and 'leapfrog', and memorable phrases like 'tower of strength', 'cruel to be kind', and 'method

PORTRAIT OF A QUEEN

This iconic picture of Elizabeth standing on her kingdom is by Marcus Gheeraerts and is considered to be the finest portrait of the queen during her lifetime. It was commissioned by the leading courtier Sir Henry Lee, who lived at Ditchley, Oxfordshire, and it is therefore known as the 'Ditchley' portrait.

in his madness'. Shakespeare was a major participant in the English Renaissance and made a massive contribution towards the foundation of the professional theatre as an art form.

✦

During Elizabeth's reign, the nation's religious life was completely transformed by the change from Roman Catholicism to Protestantism and the establishment of the Anglican Church. The Church of England, however, came under considerable pressure from the more extreme Puritans, and a titanic struggle ensued between them, which was still unresolved at the time of the queen's death.

THE MODERN GLOBE

An authentic replica of Shakespeare's theatre built on virtually the same site as the original Globe on the South Bank of the River Thames in London. Here audiences can experience theatre-going as it was in Shakespeare's day.

The nation emerged as a maritime power, enabling it to participate belatedly in the exploration of the world and to discover new horizons, so enhancing trade, commerce and the nation's wealth, and leading to the creation of a worldwide empire. Because of its skilful sea captains and superior ships, England was able to successfully confront Spain, the European superpower, defeating it in one of the most decisive sea battles in the nation's history.

Elizabethan England also had its dark side. Roman Catholics were ruthlessly persecuted. The use of torture on political prisoners in the Tower of London was officially authorized, and public executions, when those convicted were hanged, drawn and quartered, were brutal.

THE ARMADA IS IN SIGHT

This dramatic Victorian engraving, after the style of John Seymour Lucas, shows Sir Francis Drake playing bowls on Plymouth Hoe as a messenger arrives with news of the approaching Armada. This historic work hangs in Buckland Abbey, a few miles north of Plymouth and Drake's home in Elizabethan times.

ELIZABETHAN GRANDEUR

The east front of Burton Constable in East Yorkshire, which was built in the 16th century by Sir John Constable and is still lived in by the Constable family. It is a fine example of a grand Elizabethan residence.

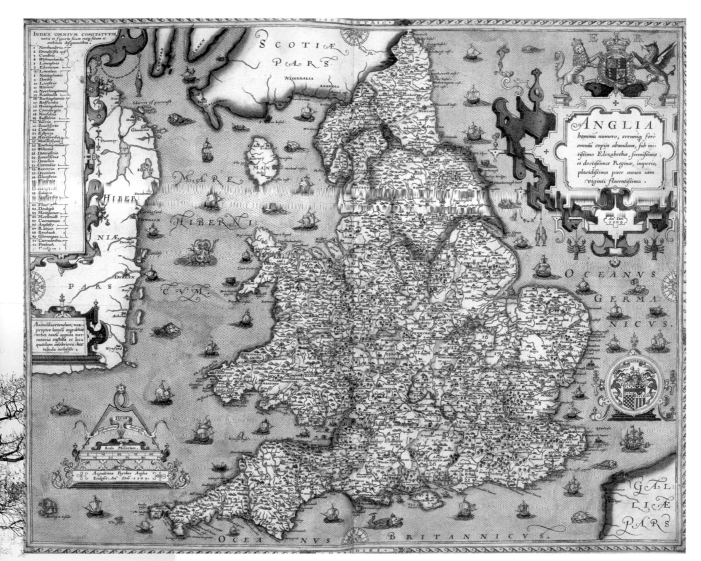

The large-scale increase in poverty throughout the kingdom was ineffectively dealt with by Elizabeth's government, whereas the growth of materialism and the desire to impress at all costs rose to obsessive levels amongst the elite and the rapidly growing, more affluent middle classes.

Despite these shortcomings, Elizabethan England was admired and respected by most of the known world. Shakespeare expressed the national mood in *Richard II*: 'This royal throne of kings, this scepter'd isle, This earth of majesty'. Four centuries later, people are still as dazzled and delighted.

THE ELIZABETHAN KINGDOM

A contemporary map of England and Wales in the late 16th century, when Scotland was an independent kingdom and Ireland the nation's first overseas colony. Although Elizabeth's grandfather, Henry VII, had been born in Wales, the queen never visited the country.

ELIZABETH, THE EARLY YEARS

ENTRANCE TO HAMPTON
COURT PALACE

*Hampton Court Palace greatly
impressed visitors: 'the most
splendid and most magnificent
to be found in England, or for
that matter other countries',
declared the excited Duke of
Wurttemberg in 1592.*

ELIZABETH'S FATHER

*Hans Eworth's copy of Holbein's
portrait of Henry VIII at Trinity
College, Cambridge, founded by
Henry in 1546. This picture
conveys a powerful, intimidating
man with an air of menace.*

ELIZABETH GREW UP IN turbulent times
and she suffered considerable personal
trauma. She had an emotionally unstable
father, who had her mother executed, an
unhappy and resentful half-sister and a
religious fanatic as a half-brother – the
ultimate dysfunctional family. The nation
was racked by religious turmoil, threatened by civil war and invasion. But
Elizabeth's experiences forged qualities
that enabled her to become one of
history's greatest monarchs.

The new queen's initial period on the
throne proved equally eventful. Elizabeth
fell in love for probably the only time in
her life, yet unlike her father King Henry,
she never let her heart rule her head
but coolly considered marriage options
purely for political purposes. Having
rejected countless suitors, Elizabeth came
close to marrying a very unlikely French
candidate. Meanwhile, she conducted a
long-running, long-range duel with her
glamorous cousin, Mary Queen of Scots.

Amidst the frantic upheaval of a
European religious revolution, she slowly
but surely reintroduced Protestantism,
initiated by her half-brother Edward VI
but reversed by her half-sister Mary I.
Elizabeth permanently established the
Anglican church. As Roman Catholics,
Lutherans and Calvinists – originators
of the phrase 'born-again Christians' –
scrambled for the moral high ground, she

skilfully charted a middle course between
old style Roman Catholicism and the
new, more extreme evangelicalism.

Elizabeth was not the first female
monarch to achieve power; nevertheless
she was the first with the attributes neces-
sary to exercise it for the benefit of her
kingdom. She carefully observed the
world around her and learned accordingly. She listened to the advice of her
well-chosen Privy Council. She was
cautious, never made a hasty decision,
and, if occasionally she made a mistake,
was quick to recognize and correct it.
Above all, a reputation first established in
these early years has survived more than
four centuries.

ELIZABETH'S MOTHER

*Anne Boleyn's portrait by an
unknown artist hangs in the
National Portrait Gallery in
London. She was only 29 years
old when accused of adultery
and incest with her half-brother
and then executed.*

A ROYAL CHILD IS BORN

A FAVOURITE PALACE

Greenwich Palace was rebuilt by Henry VII, Elizabeth's grandfather. Like many of the royal palaces it was sited on the banks of the River Thames to afford easy access by royal barge.

YOUNG PRINCESS

This is the earliest identifiable portrait of Elizabeth, probably painted when she was about 12 or 13 years old. The books, one in her hand and one by her side, show her as a serious scholar.

ELIZABETH WAS BORN on an autumnal Sunday afternoon in 1533 at Greenwich Palace, the birthplace of her father, Henry VIII, 42 years earlier. It was a normal birth, mother and child doing well. Elizabeth was a bonny baby with her father's distinctive auburn hair, yet Henry was not happy. He had longed for a son, a male heir to inherit his kingdom. He had not divorced Catherine, his wife of 24 years, to marry the flirtatious Anne Boleyn and incur the wrath of Rome, merely to produce another daughter. The announcement of the arrival of a prince was hurriedly altered to that of a princess; plans for elaborate celebrations were abandoned. The king felt foolish – were

his courtiers laughing at him behind his ample back? Henry was well aware that Anne was unpopular and that there was considerable sympathy for Catherine, both at Court and throughout the English kingdom.

When Elizabeth was three, her father had her mother executed. The young princess was declared illegitimate and banished from Court. She began a nomadic journey between various isolated country houses, while her father embarked on a matrimonial odyssey with a series of wives. It is not surprising that Elizabeth remembered her father and emphasized her descent from him, yet never mentioned her mother, whom she scarcely saw.

HATFIELD OLD PALACE

The old Tudor palace in Hertfordshire was given to Elizabeth by her father and she spent a great deal of time here prior to becoming queen. This is where she held her first Privy Council meeting.

Henry took only a passing interest in his younger daughter; nevertheless he did ensure that she received an excellent education from two of the finest scholars in the land, William Grindal and Roger Asham. The latter's relationship with Elizabeth lasted until his death in 1568 from a serious chill. Asham combined academic excellence with a passion for gambling, an interest he passed on to Elizabeth, along with a sound knowledge of Latin and Greek. The princess was a gifted and dedicated pupil, particularly for languages, also learning French, Spanish, Flemish and Italian, even some Welsh. Both her tutors were ardent Protestants and their religious views greatly influenced the impressionable young princess.

Elizabeth's visits to Court were infrequent. They were mainly for state occasions such as the baptism of her half-brother Edward, the son produced at last by Henry's third wife, Jane Seymour, who treated Elizabeth kindly and helped to reunite Henry with his younger daughter. Thereafter, although Henry continued to change wives, Elizabeth became part of the royal family once again. The king's fourth wife, Anne of Cleves, took Elizabeth riding, an activity she adored and enjoyed for the rest of her life.

Elizabeth's relationship with the sexy, yet stupid, Catherine Howard, however, was short-lived as Henry's fifth wife soon followed Elizabeth's mother Anne Boleyn to the scaffold. Perhaps the fate of Henry's many wives influenced Elizabeth's view of marriage: marital bliss appearing to be merely transitory.

When Henry took Catherine Parr to be his sixth wife Elizabeth was brought back to Court and her life became more stable. This happy state of affairs did not last for long. Three years later, in the early hours of 28 January 1547, Henry VIII died. Thereafter Elizabeth's path to the throne was destined to become extremely perilous.

ELIZABETH'S HALF-BROTHER

Edward was Henry's son by Jane Seymour, his third wife, who died in childbirth. William Scrots' portrait of Prince Edward depicts his attempt to imitate his father's swaggering pose. Edward VI succeeded Henry VIII in 1547 but his health was not strong and he died in 1553.

A PRINCESS IN PERIL

SOON AFTER HENRY VIII died, Catherine Parr, widowed for a third time, married Lord Thomas Seymour, the highly ambitious uncle of the young King Edward VI. Elizabeth, by then a vivacious teenager, went to live with the newly-weds at their house in Chelsea. Seymour was tall, dark and very handsome, just the sort of man calculated to appeal to Elizabeth. A mutual attraction soon developed and Seymour began to visit Elizabeth's bedroom early in the day, still in his nightshirt and before she was dressed. Seymour, more than twice Elizabeth's age, chased her around the room, kissing and cuddling her, as the young princess shrieked and giggled with pleasure. Amazingly Seymour's wife, Catherine, also joined in these suggestive games.

This rather sordid affair only ended when Catherine caught Elizabeth and Seymour in a passionate embrace. Elizabeth was banished to Cheshunt in Hertfordshire. The shameful incident later became public knowledge when Seymour was charged with high treason and Elizabeth found herself interrogated by Sir Robert Tyrwhitt, the Privy Council's Special Commissioner. This embarrassing occurrence taught Elizabeth a salutary lesson on the importance of discretion.

After her half-brother Edward died in 1553, Mary inherited the throne. Elizabeth initially enjoyed an amicable relationship with her Roman Catholic half-sister, riding into London with her and attending her coronation.

'I stood in danger of my life, my sister was so incensed against me.' Elizabeth I

The L. Elizabeth before her Sister Q. Mary

ELIZABETH IN DANGER

Elizabeth meekly kneels in supplication before her half-sister, Mary. Elizabeth could easily have been executed for treason – so she had to be extremely careful.

TAKEN TO THE TOWER

Early on the morning of 18 March 1554, two of Mary's senior Privy Councillors, the Marquess of Winchester and the Earl of Sussex, came to Whitehall Palace to escort Elizabeth to the Tower. She was taken downstream on the River Thames by barge. It was a dark and dreary day, rain pouring from a leaden sky. The streets were deserted – it was Palm Sunday and everyone was in church. The swirling tide made it difficult to pass under London Bridge, increasing Elizabeth's anxiety. When they finally arrived at Tower Wharf she clambered out of the barge, slumped down on the wet flagstones and refused to move. Never had she felt so threatened or alone. **'Let us use such dealings that we may answer it thereafter,'** cautioned Sussex. Wise words – Elizabeth survived to become queen and appointed both Sussex and Winchester to her first Privy Council.

THE BELL TOWER

It was here in the Tower of London that Elizabeth was imprisoned in 1554 on the orders of her half-sister Queen Mary. This tower was ominously close to Tower Green, the scene of many executions including that of Elizabeth's mother Anne Boleyn.

QUEEN AND CONSORT

This portrait of Queen Mary and her husband Philip of Spain hangs in the Long Gallery at Woburn Abbey, Bedfordshire. When Mary died and Elizabeth became queen, Philip, by then king of Spain, immediately proposed to her.

Mary's decision to marry Philip of Spain proved to be extremely unpopular, however. It sparked an armed uprising in Kent led by Sir Thomas Wyatt, a local squire, who then proceeded to march on London. The revolt was soon suppressed and Wyatt arrested, but letters were discovered apparently implicating Elizabeth in the plot – Wyatt's intention being to remove Mary from the throne and replace her with Elizabeth. The young princess suddenly found herself in mortal danger as a vengeful Queen Mary ordered her half-sister to be imprisoned in the Tower of London, where her mother, Anne Boleyn, had been executed 18 years previously. Was Elizabeth about to share the same fate? Summoned to appear before Mary at Hampton Court Palace, however, Elizabeth was able to convince her half-sister of her innocence and secure her release from the Tower.

BECOMING A QUEEN

QUEEN ELIZABETH'S GREATEST LOVE

Sir Robert Dudley, later Earl of Leicester. This portrait by Steven van der Meulen can be found in the Wallace Collection in London. A fiery romance faded into a warm friendship and the queen was greatly saddened when he died.

CHIEF MINISTER

Marcus Gheeraerts' portrait of Lord Burghley hangs in Burghley House, his home in East Anglia. He served the queen wisely and faithfully for most of her reign.

IN 1558 THE UNHAPPY MARY died, possibly from a tumour, having belatedly and reluctantly acknowledged her half-sister as the rightful heir. The kingdom of England was in a parlous state when Elizabeth came to the throne: 'the queen poor, the realm exhausted, the nobility poor and decayed'. The new monarch faced a daunting challenge; fortunately she was determined, conscientious and hard working with an instinctive grasp of the art of leadership, knowing exactly how to inspire her subjects. Elizabeth possessed a wonderful ability to pick capable men to help govern her kingdom, particularly key ministers for her Privy Council, such as William Cecil, later Lord Burghley, who served her for virtually her entire reign. Queen in a man's world, she used her gender to advantage, to charm, cajole and manipulate for her own benefit. Her man-management skills were masterly, particularly when 'fishing for men's souls', as Sir Christopher Hatton so memorably declared.

The new queen radiated charm and authority. She was astute, articulate and highly intelligent. She was also cautious, an ultra conservative monarch in a rapidly changing world, slow to make up her mind, exceedingly quick to change it. She was very adept at shifting blame elsewhere if her popularity was threatened. Elizabeth had inherited her father's fiery temper, and was capable of violent and unpredictable mood swings. At times she could be maddeningly indecisive, yet throughout her reign she maintained the loyalty of her council and the love of her subjects. Elizabeth was a people's queen with a flair for public relations and was always extremely conscious of her image.

Elizabeth was tall, auburn haired and vivacious, attractive without being particularly beautiful. 'Her face is comely rather than handsome, but she is tall and well formed; with a good skin, although sallow; she has fine eyes,' commented the Venetian ambassador Giovanni Michiel, shortly before Elizabeth came to the throne.

'They say that she is in love with Lord Robert and never lets him leave her.'

de Feria, Spanish Ambassador

DANCING THE NIGHT AWAY

This lively picture of the queen dancing the volta with Robert Dudley hangs in Penshurst Place in Kent, the home of Sir Philip Sidney, the charismatic Elizabethan courtier and poet.

She displayed the same commanding presence as her father Henry VIII, a quality quickly noted by the Court. She was an extrovert whereas the previous queen, her half-sister Mary, had been rather shy. Where Mary had been dowdy and dull, Elizabeth positively glowed. In short, she had star quality. Her courtiers were captivated, her subjects enchanted.

The new queen was also in love, the focus of her affection the hugely handsome Robert Dudley, who she had created Master of Horse shortly after ascending the throne.

DELIGHTFUL YET DANGEROUS

It soon became obvious to the Court that Elizabeth and Dudley were infatuated with each other. The passionate and public nature of their affair shocked her courtiers, particularly as Dudley was married and had the reputation of being a serial seducer. Tongues wagged throughout the kingdom and across Europe: **'The Queen of England is going to marry her horse keeper,'** jeered Mary Queen of Scots. Elizabeth did not care. After many years of tedium and tension, all her pent-up emotions had exploded into a glorious romance. Elizabeth gave little thought to the implications of this dangerous liaison or where it might lead. She was enjoying herself. She was ecstatically happy. She was in love.

THE RIVAL QUEENS

'Alas the poor fool, they will never cease until she loses her head. They will put her to death, it is her own fault and folly.'

Charles IX, King of France

A TRAGIC QUEEN

A young Mary Queen of Scots, depicted in a miniature by the French artist Clouet, painted c.1558 and now part of the Royal Collection. It usually hangs in the Palace of Holyroodhouse, Edinburgh. Mary was executed when 45 years old, having spent nearly half of her life in captivity.

ELIZABETH NEVER MET her cousin, Mary Queen of Scots, but they exchanged fond letters: 'so tender a cousin and friend'. Meetings were arranged, only to be cancelled when overtaken by events. The time never seemed opportune. Elizabeth distrusted Mary, a Roman Catholic with designs on the English throne – to which some said Mary had a better claim than Elizabeth, also being descended from Elizabeth's grandfather, Henry VII. Mary was younger than her English cousin and considered to be more attractive. Certainly she was the cause of much concern for Elizabeth, a state of affairs that steadily worsened as time progressed.

Mary returned to her native Scotland in 1561 after the death of her first husband, the French king François II. Initially Elizabeth tried to be kind to her fellow queen, yet Mary possessed an unfailing ability to irritate Elizabeth, either with her provocative attitude or ill-considered, impetuous actions. Typical of the latter was her impulsive marriage to the vain Lord Darnley, soon to be murdered by the Scottish noble

MARY'S DEATH WARRANT

The Privy Council's letter ordering the execution of Mary Queen of Scots, dated 3 February 1587, is now in the library of Lambeth Palace in London. Its signatories include the Earl of Leicester and Lord Burghley.

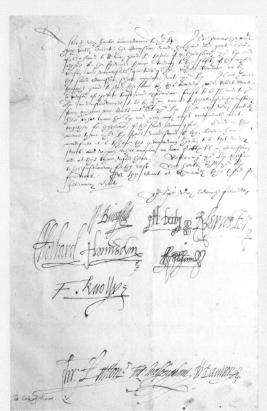

Lord Bothwell – possibly with Mary's connivance. Mary then shocked everybody by marrying him! An army led by Scottish nobles confronted Mary and Bothwell; Mary was captured and forced to abdicate. She fled across the Solway Firth to England.

The sudden arrival of this royal refugee gave the English queen a considerable problem. Elizabeth was initially inclined to invite her cousin to Court but was quickly dissuaded by her council, who recognized the threat that Mary posed as a focal point for Roman Catholic insurgency. 'The Queen of Scots is and always shall be a dangerous person to your estate,' warned Cecil. So it proved, Mary rashly allowing herself to be used in intrigues against Elizabeth and a succession of amateurish plots which were quickly detected. Meanwhile Elizabeth contemplated a

ROYAL NEEDLEWORK

This lovely piece of embroidery was skilfully created by Mary Queen of Scots and is now displayed at the Palace of Holyroodhouse, Mary's royal palace when she was on the Scottish throne. The cat is said to represent Elizabeth and the mouse Mary.

THE ENGLISH QUEEN

Elizabeth's portrait, c.1599 by Rowland Lockey, an apprentice of Nicholas Hilliard, hangs in the Long Gallery at Hardwick Hall in Derbyshire close to one of Mary Queen of Scots. The two queens never met, nor visited Hardwick Hall.

number of increasingly bizarre ways to rid herself of her unwelcome guest: bribe the Scots to have her back, even have Mary quietly exterminated.

Finally, after 18 years of comfortable custody, Mary exhausted Elizabeth's patience. Very reluctantly she agreed to her cousin's trial and execution for treason.

Mary was a Catholic queen in Presbyterian Scotland who fled to Protestant England: her death made her a Roman Catholic martyr. She was gullible, misguided and isolated, a victim of circumstance, yet she certainly contributed to her own demise. 'I am my own executioner,' wrote John Donne – it could have been a fitting epitaph for the tragic Mary Queen of Scots.

17

MATTHEW PARKER

Lambeth Palace in London houses this fine portrait of Elizabeth's first Archbishop of Canterbury. He was reluctant to take the post and deliberated for six months before accepting.

WHEN ELIZABETH INHERITED the throne, a religious reformation was sweeping across Europe, the old order challenged by new religious doctrines. The new queen was well aware that she was expected to restore the Protestant faith to her kingdom. Elizabeth was a devout follower of the 'new religion', yet was very conscious of the difficulties involved and determined to avoid extremism. The nation she inherited had been Roman Catholic for many centuries – much of the Midlands and the North remained so. Elizabeth was determined to pursue a moderate course and respect other beliefs: 'not make windows into men's souls', according to Francis Bacon. This enabled England to avoid the vicious religious wars prevalent in France and, when the King of Spain finally attacked, most English Roman Catholics remained loyal. Fortunately for Elizabeth the Roman Catholic Archbishop of Canterbury, Cardinal Reginald Pole, had died the same year as Queen Mary, leaving the way clear for a Protestant replacement. She persuaded the shy and scholarly Matthew Parker to leave the cloistered calm of Cambridge, where he had been Vice-Chancellor, to oversee her kingdom's religious reform. This proved an excellent choice: Parker was indeed mild mannered yet possessed the tact and tenacity to establish Protestantism despite considerable opposition from Roman Catholic bishops and nobility. A number of acts of parliament were passed, albeit with difficulty, and obstructive bishops were replaced by ones more sympathetic to the Protestant cause.

When Parker died in 1575, the queen was persuaded to appoint Edmund Grindal as his successor – a big mistake, as Grindal proved too sympathetic to the Puritans, allowing them to preach their beliefs openly. He was confined to Lambeth Palace by an irate queen, took no further meaningful role in the nation's religious affairs and died six years later. Elizabeth's third Archbishop was far more to her liking and she nicknamed him 'my little black husband'. John Whitgift successfully upheld the authority of the Anglican Church in the face of a growing challenge from the Puritans. Tough and resourceful, he silenced the vocal Presbyterian leader Thomas Cartwright, suppressed the hostile Puritan press and outwitted pro-Puritan Privy Councillors.

AN EMBARRASSING ENCOUNTER

Perceived wisdom in 16th-century England said that clergy should remain unmarried and celibate and any existing wives should be kept out of sight. It was said that the wife of Thomas Cranmer, Archbishop of Canterbury in the reign of Henry VIII, travelled around the kingdom concealed in a large trunk. When Elizabeth unexpectedly visited Lambeth Palace she was surprised to meet Margaret Parker, the wife of her first archbishop. The queen was unusually flustered:

'Madam I may not call you; mistress I am ashamed to call you; so I know not what to call you, but howsoever, I thank you,' she stammered.

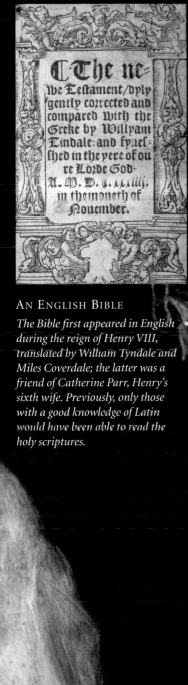

AN ENGLISH BIBLE

The Bible first appeared in English during the reign of Henry VIII, translated by William Tyndale and Miles Coverdale; the latter was a friend of Catherine Parr, Henry's sixth wife. Previously, only those with a good knowledge of Latin would have been able to read the holy scriptures.

Roman Catholicism remained a problem, particularly as relationships with Spain deteriorated and Jesuits, members of The Society of Jesus, secretly entered the country to offer the sacrament to Catholics and discourage them from attending Protestant services, regardless of the consequences. Robert Southwell and Edmund Campion were among the 100 or more Roman Catholic martyrs tortured and executed during the second half of Elizabeth's reign. By the time the queen's life drew to a close the Church of England had been firmly established with sufficiently strong foundations to last to present times: arguably, this was Elizabeth's finest achievement.

'MY LITTLE BLACK HUSBAND'

This was the nickname given by Elizabeth to her third Archbishop, John Whitgift, the only member of the Church ever to be an Elizabethan Privy Councillor. Whitgift was with her at her deathbed.

A MARRIAGE PROPOSAL

THE PRIVY COUNCIL and parliament pestered Elizabeth to choose a husband from the moment she became queen in order to produce a healthy son and secure the Tudor succession. Elizabeth was reluctant to oblige. She was a successful career woman, enjoyed ruling her kingdom and had no intention of sharing it with anyone. 'I will have here but one mistress and no master,' she famously screamed at her long time favourite Robert Dudley, in front of the Court.

Elizabeth's observations of married life left her unimpressed. She had seen her father, Henry VIII, assiduously rearranging his love life, while his attitude to marriage brought a whole new meaning to the phrase 'until death do us part', as her mother, Anne Boleyn, had discovered to her cost. Elizabeth's half-sister, Mary, had made an unhappy marriage, while her cousin, Mary Queen of Scots, experienced two marital disasters. The thought of taking a husband had little appeal – it could lose you your kingdom, or even your head. Nevertheless, to please her Privy Council the queen dutifully went through the motions of courtship. It flattered her ego to be pursued by so many eminent suitors – even though they all proved to be unsuitable.

Most of the crowned heads of Europe wooed her and lost. Her councillors had reconciled themselves to never hearing the sound of royal wedding bells, let alone the patter of princely feet. Then in 1581 an

'MY LITTLE FROG'

The king of France's younger brother came close to marrying the queen in 1581. Having initially agreed the match, Elizabeth perceived the Court's disapproval, so made exorbitant conditions which she knew the French king would never accept.

LOVE STORY

'On the 22nd however, at eleven in the morning, the queen and Alençon were walking together in a gallery, Leicester and Walsingham being present, when the French ambassador entered and said that he wished to write to his master, from whom he had received orders to hear from the queen's own lips, her intention with regards to marrying his brother. She replied, **"You may write this to the King: that the Duke of Alençon shall be my husband"** and at the same time she turned to Alençon and kissed him on the mouth, drawing a ring from her own hand and giving it to him as a pledge ....' So wrote Mendoza, the Spanish Ambassador, in a letter to King Philip.

unexpected suitor reappeared in the diminutive shape of the Duke of Alençon, brother of the king of France and youngest son of Catherine de Medici, the real power behind the French throne. The Court was amazed – the duke was not at all the sort of man that normally attracted Elizabeth. Besides being small, he had a very large nose, a face heavily pock-marked from smallpox, and was nearly half her age. Her royal courtiers were even more bemused when the queen pronounced him enchanting and nick-named him 'my little frog'.

In reality this was more a case of 'realpolitik' than a royal romance. Relationships between England and Spain were steadily worsening and King Philip had annexed Portugal, whose fleet consider-ably enhanced Spanish sea power. A meaningful alliance with France was urgently required: what better way to seal it than with a traditional royal wedding?

THE ELIZABETHAN KINGDOM

ELIZABETH'S KINGDOM underwent profound changes during her 45 years as monarch, affecting the entire nation and all its subjects in every aspect of their lives. England's population doubled during the 16th century and, by the end of the queen's reign, one in every five of her subjects lived in towns, as industry, trade and commerce rapidly began to replace agriculture as the most common source of employment.

Education improved enormously: many grammar schools were founded during Elizabeth's reign and opportunities for learning were greatly enhanced. The discovery of the New World and other hitherto unexplored territories led to the availability of much new and exotic food. On the other hand, medicine, transport and communications improved little and there was still no organized police force or fire brigade. The lack of development in these areas had a deleterious effect on a rapidly increasing population.

Elizabethans became progressively more materialistic. Ambition and avarice went hand in hand and enterprise quickly led to excess. The English stately home made its first appearance, the garden became a place for pleasure rather than just for producing food, and clothing had to be fashionable rather than merely wearable.

Elizabethans were highly energetic: they worked hard and played hard. A wedding or the birth of a child was the perfect excuse for family and friends to celebrate far into the night and through the following day. Elizabethan England was a wonderful place provided you were not out of favour with the queen, a Roman Catholic, unemployed, very poor or seriously ill.

ELIZABETHAN TOWNS AND VILLAGES

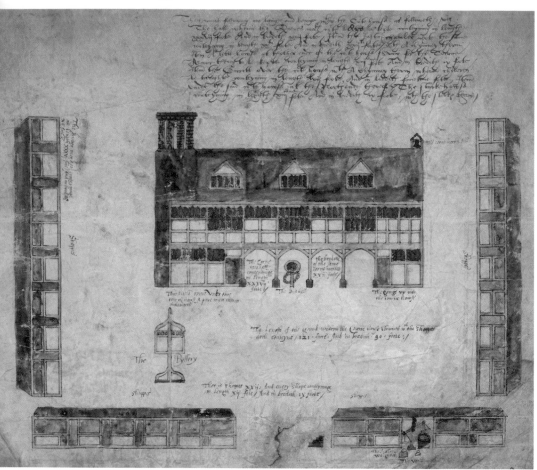

THE URBANIZATION OF England increased during Elizabeth's reign, as the migration of people from countryside to town in search of work and fresh opportunities gathered pace. Nowhere was this more evident than in London, where the population, which approached 200,000 towards the end of the 16th century, was destined to double during the following 50 years. Elsewhere, Norwich, Bristol, Plymouth and York had sizeable populations, yet the number of people living in the average town remained quite modest. Stratford-upon-Avon, a thriving market town, contained some 2,000 citizens in Shakespeare's time, its buildings far more widely spread than today, with extensive gardens and orchards throughout the town.

AN ELIZABETHAN MARKET

Although new shops were constantly opening, the regular market still remained the essential place for buying and selling goods, and meeting friends and neighbours to exchange the latest gossip.

ELIZABETHAN SEA CAPTAIN'S HOUSE

The narrow, winding, cobbled New Street on Plymouth's Barbican contains a number of original Elizabethan houses. The one on the right with latticed windows is a former Elizabethan sea captain's house, now a museum portraying life in 16th-century Plymouth.

The outward appearance of Elizabethan towns and villages, with their attractive half-timbered exteriors, appeared very picturesque but concealed a multitude of disadvantages. There was no running water and sanitation was extremely poor. There were no proper drains and all manner of rubbish was thrown into the streets and left to rot. Inevitably such lack of hygiene led to a wide range of dangerous diseases, particularly bubonic plague and typhus. The number of deaths in London during an average year exceeded births, the growth in population being entirely due to the influx of people seeking a better life. Buildings constructed of wood, straw and other highly flammable materials constantly led to serious fires. Three large-scale outbreaks occurred in Stratford during Shakespeare's lifetime.

༄

Regular markets remained an important part of life, a celebrated one being held in the nave of St Paul's Cathedral in London. The number of individual shops grew considerably throughout Elizabethan England, many run by enterprising women, whilst numerous stallholders and street vendors were also female. Trade and commerce thrived in the towns, controlled by the all-powerful guilds. Inns provided both a resting place for travellers and a social centre, where townsfolk could eat and drink beer and sack, a sherry-type wine that was especially popular with thirsty Elizabethans.

༄

For those arriving from the country for the first time, London was a considerable cultural shock. It was overcrowded, noisy, dirty, heavily polluted and full of noxious smells. As there was no street lighting, the city could be a hazardous place to walk at night; lawlessness abounded. In summer there was a constant risk of plague. In winter, the city was invariably blanketed in thick fog and, when the River Thames froze over, ice fairs were held on it. London Bridge was the only bridge across the river. More than 300 metres (900 feet) long, with shops and wealthy merchants' houses along its entire length, it was much admired by visitors: it was 'the most beautiful bridge in the world', according to Frenchman Etienne Perlin. London spilled out beyond the walls of the original medieval city with sprawling suburbs engulfing villages and countryside. It was, however, a vibrant, exciting place where enterprise could be rewarded. This was the pulsating cauldron of a city where Shakespeare came in search of a new life. He certainly found it.

ELIZABETHAN BAKERY
Entitled The Ordinance of the Bakers of York, *the guild that controlled the making of bread in that city, this picture shows a baker and his apprentice at work.*

IN THE STOCKS
A 16th-century woodcut conveys the public shame of being found guilty of a minor misdemeanour: the culprit was placed in the stocks and pelted with rubbish by jeering citizens.

'When daisies pied and violets blue
And lady-smocks all silver-white
And cuckoo-buds of yellow hue
Do paint the meadows with delight.'

William Shakespeare, Love's Labours Lost

WILLIAM SHAKESPEARE'S ROMANTIC view of
the 16th-century English countryside
mirrors a modern city-dweller's nostalgia
for idyllic pastoral delights. In reality life
in Elizabethan rural England was far
harsher than Shakespeare's sentimental
childhood memories. The average coun-
tryman endured unremitting toil from
dawn to dusk, six days a week, in order to
maintain his family. Their lives were occasionally brightened by annual fairs and
wandering groups of musicians or actors –
Shakespeare's company toured as far west
as Barnstaple in North Devon.

England was still an agricultural nation,
but the traditional farming practices of
the Middle Ages were changing with the
introduction of improved methods of
husbandry and new crops, such as hops,
potatoes and turnips. More and more
common land was enclosed to become
the property of wealthy landowners.

There was a continual growth in
Continental demand for English cloth,
which led to progressively more land
being converted from arable farming
to sheep rearing. Cloth-producing mills
sprang up in the Cotswolds and in other
areas which are now of outstanding natu-
ral beauty. Industrial development was
beginning to scar the Elizabethan countryside: coal mining and iron works in
the Weald of Kent and the Forest of Dean,
cloth manufacturing in East Anglia, the
Cotswolds and Wiltshire.

A COUNTRY WOMAN

This picture illustrates the differ-
ence in clothing for a woman
in the country as opposed to at
Court. The emphasis is very
much on comfort and practical-
ity rather than on fashion.

HARVEST TIME

This pen and brown ink on
paper drawing is entitled
Landscape with Harvesters
Returning Home. *It dates from*
1595–1605 and represents a
typical example of farming at
the end of the 16th century.

COUNTRY LIFE

This Bradford table carpet, now to be found in the Victoria and Albert Museum in London, features rural life in the late 16th century with a watermill and hunting with dogs.

Woodland, which had traditionally covered much of the land, was rapidly disappearing as trees were felled for building houses and ships and for smelting in the production of iron. However much wooded area remained, such as the Forest of Arden around Stratford-upon-Avon, the inspiration for many of the settings for Shakespeare's plays. Furthermore the growth of industrialization had yet to impair traditional craftsmanship, particularly in building, so original humble farmworkers' cottages are much prized in today's property market.

Communications in the 16th-century countryside had improved little since the Middle Ages. Although it was the responsibility of local landowners to maintain the roads most failed to do so, resulting in dusty tracks in summer that became impassably muddy in winter. The English wayside inns, however, were rated some of the best in Europe. The main form of transport was still horseback. Horse-drawn carriages had been introduced from Holland in 1564 but, being unsprung, they were exceedingly uncomfortable. The only alternative was river boat. Travel was tedious, time-consuming and, in sparsely populated countryside, extremely hazardous – armed robbers often lay in wait for unwary travellers.

In spite of these difficulties the working-class population was surprisingly mobile, travelling around in search of fresh employment. Like the rest of the nation, the Elizabethan countryside was a vibrant place; subject to profound change, country folk were robust, resourceful, adaptable and capable of facing up to any new challenge.

DESIGNER LABEL

The bay window in the north-east corner of Little Moreton Hall in Cheshire has the name of the carpenter, Richard Dale, proudly carved upon it. Dale's carpentry is a fine example of Elizabethan craftsmanship.

ELIZABETHAN PRODIGY HOUSES

'More like a town than a house … the towers and pinnacles like so many distant parish churches.'

Daniel Defoe's description of Burghley House

THE ULTIMATE STATUS SYMBOL in Elizabethan England was the prodigy house: huge, ostentatious and assertive, clearly demonstrating to all the world that its owner was wealthy, successful and very important. Lord Burghley's house near Stamford in Lincolnshire had taken the queen's most eminent and trusted minister more than 30 years to complete. It compelled the admiration of visitors, such as the novelist Daniel Defoe, who were overwhelmed by its forest of towers, obelisks and pinnacles.

Many of these enormous new houses, including Burghley, Burton Constable, Longleat, Hardwick Hall and Montacute, were built in Renaissance style – the latest architecture – unlike today, when most large new homes are constructed in a neo-Palladian image rather than contemporary design. Thrustful Elizabethan owners had courage and vision and were determined to display their cultural credentials. Burghley, Burton Constable and Longleat remain in the hands of the same families who built them some 400 years ago, and

MAGNIFICENT ENGLISH RENAISSANCE HOUSE

Sir John Thynne, owner of Longleat in Wiltshire, succeeded where Bess of Hardwick failed, for he entertained the queen at his home in 1574. Today, the façade of Longleat appears much as it did at the time of her visit.

BESS OF HARDWICK

Although inscribed as a portrait of Mary Queen of Scots, this picture at Hardwick Hall is now thought to be the only portrait which features Bess as a youthful beauty.

continue to be admired by the countless visitors who go to see them every year.

The key features of an Elizabethan prodigy house were its sheer scale and visibility. Size was everything: tall chimneys, massive windows, sweeping façades, soaring gables. It was often constructed on the top of a hill, not to view more of the countryside but to be more easily seen by envious neighbours or impressionable travellers. Most prodigy houses were created for owners with newly acquired fortunes who wished everyone to be aware of their success. Inside were spectacular staircases, long galleries disappearing into the distance, and a Great Hall of awesome proportions. Big was undoubtedly beautiful in the Elizabethan age, where ego fuelled ambition and wealth was the ultimate prize. The Elizabethan era was one of opulence, exuberance and extravagance, fully reflected in prodigy houses, the first English stately homes.

BESS OF HARDWICK

Bess rose from relative obscurity via four progressively richer husbands to become the wealthiest woman, and one of the most influential, in England after the queen. Following the death of her last husband, the 6th Earl of Shrewsbury, Bess began to build Hardwick Hall, still regarded as one of the nation's greatest historical houses. It would be wrong to judge Bess purely on her ability to attract men with money, for she was an eminently successful entrepreneur in her own right: **'She was a builder, a buyer and seller of estates,** a money lender, a farmer and a merchant of lead, coals and timber,' wrote the admiring Edmund Lodge in *Illustrations of British History*. Her portrait in the Long Gallery at Hardwick shows a proud, forceful and ambitious lady, determined to have her own way. Bess survived into her 80s, outliving the queen by five years. Today her initials remain proudly carved on top of the towers of the great prodigy house she created so many years ago.

ELIZABETHAN GARDENS

'God Almighty first planted a garden; and, indeed, it is the purest of human pleasures. It is the greatest refreshment of the spirit of man.'

Francis Bacon, Essays

GLORIOUS GAZEBO

The gardens at Montacute House in Somerset contain a pair of stylish gazebos, which were an important feature of Elizabethan garden design. Built in local honey-coloured Ham stone, they date from the end of the 16th century.

IN THE ELIZABETHAN ERA the garden became a place to enjoy, not just a plot of land for growing herbs and vegetables. The Elizabethan garden provided somewhere to walk, to play games, and to sit and contemplate the beauties of nature. The lawn had been developed largely to provide a suitable surface for playing bowls, an increasingly popular pastime in 16th-century England. The queen is reputed to have played with Francis Drake at Berkeley Castle in Gloucestershire, where the smooth turf in the garden beneath the castle battlements is now known as Elizabeth's Bowling Green.

The Elizabethan garden was exceedingly formal in appearance with well-trimmed topiary. The elaborate knot was a key feature: formal beds planted with low hedges of box or yew to form regular patterns, either 'open' with sand or gravel or 'closed' with contrasting planting. Whilst no original 16th-century garden exists in England, excellent examples have been recreated at Hampton Court Palace, Staffordshire's Moseley Old Hall and Little Moreton Hall in Cheshire, which combines knot and topiary.

Gazebos were also popular for dining, drinking, gambling and late-night romantic assignations. The stylish pair at Montacute in Somerset, built towards the end of the 16th century, were known as 'pudding houses', dessert being served there after the main course had been consumed in the nearby manor house.

TOPIARY TIME

Lytes Cary in Somerset features an Elizabethan Great Hall, while the garden contains a considerable amount of yew topiary – fashionable during the second half of the 16th century and now splendidly recreated here.

AN ELIZABETHAN KNOT GARDEN

This garden at Little Moreton Hall in Cheshire is based on an Elizabethan design and has an open knot with gravel between the dwarf box hedges. Alongside are four beds planted with vegetables and herbs of the Elizabethan period.

Gardening became even more fashionable as explorers brought back exotic plants from the New World and tomatoes, asparagus and melons could be cultivated for the first time. Gardening experts began to publish instruction books, their guidance being quasi-scientific bordering on astrology. 'A gardener planting in either Taurus and Acquaries or Virgo and Pisces must as carefully take heed always that the moon is not evil-aspected,' was Thomas Hill's enigmatic advice in *The Gardener's Labyrinth*, published in 1577. Henry Lyte, 16th-century owner of the magical Lytes Cary in deepest Somerset, translated the *Niewe Herball*, first published in 1578, and dedicated it to the queen. Originally the work of Dodeons, the Flemish herbalist, it became known as the *Lytes Herbal*, and a copy can still be found at Lytes Cary, where the Elizabethan-style garden contains glorious herbaceous borders and clipped yew. Thus the Elizabethans pioneered the modern garden.

DESIGN FOR AN ELIZABETHAN GARDEN

A needlework hanging in the Victoria and Albert Museum indicates the formal nature of garden design in the Elizabethan era, with topiary, box hedging, classical statuary and an arbour.

ELIZABETHAN MEN

ENGLISHMEN WERE TRADITIONALLY said to be insular and xenophobic, suspicious and condescending towards strangers and foreigners. These national characteristics intensified during the second half of the 16th century, Elizabeth's triumph over the Armada making her subjects more patriotic and at the same time more patronizing towards visitors from abroad.

Elizabethan men were sharp dressers, particularly in the royal Court, where they strutted around like a colourful pride of peacocks in doublet and hose, huge starched ruffs, cropped cloaks and jaunty, plumed hats. An ambitious courtier spent a fortune in pursuit of the latest fashion in the hope of catching the queen's attention. Elizabeth had the reputation of being quick to notice a smart young man with a flashing smile and shapely thighs.

Further down the social scale, outfits were more practical, men more stoical – particularly in their attitude towards death, an ever present possibility. There were regular outbreaks of bubonic plague for which there was no cure, winters were much harsher than today, and the average life expectancy was only 40 years. The Grim Reaper was never far away in Elizabethan England; Shakespeare described himself as being 'in perfect health and memorie' only one month before he died.

FASHIONABLE YOUNG ELIZABETHANS

Isaac Oliver's painting of the Browne brothers in 1598 is now at Burghley House. Identically dressed, they were grandsons of the 1st Viscount Montague who was implicated in the Ridolfi Plot, a Catholic conspiracy to remove Elizabeth from the throne.

'The inhabitants are magnificently apparelled, and are exceedingly proud and overbearing.'

Jacob Rathgeb, a visitor to England in 1592

SCENE FROM A TAVERN C.1600

Popular beers of the time had bizarre names such as Huffecap, Dragon's Milk and Mad Dog. A penny would purchase a night's food and lodging at an inn.

A DOCTOR'S SURGERY

Shakespeare's elder daughter, Susanna, married a wealthy local doctor named John Hall, a Cambridge graduate. Hall's Croft, their home in the centre of Stratford, still exists and contains his surgery, complete with desk and an impressive array of decorated jars for pills and potions, together with an assortment of medical equipment. The room provides an excellent insight into medical practice during the early 17th century.

Most Elizabethan men were very superstitious, firmly believing in witches and ghosts, hence their frequent appearance in Shakespearian plays. There was plenty of law but precious little order. More than 6,000 public executions were carried out at Tyburn during Elizabeth's reign, with imprisonment or the pain and public humiliation of the pillory, stocks or ducking stool for lesser offences. Whilst Justices of the Peace were effective in administering justice, they were powerless to keep the peace without a regular professional police force, so crime remained a major problem and communities often took their own sanctions against wrong-doers.

Elizabethans were extremely litigious and the legal profession expanded greatly at this time. Trade and commerce grew considerably, too, resulting in many more merchants and the guilds becoming more powerful. A life at sea became increasingly more appealing, so in peacetime at least there was no need for press gangs to man the ships of Drake, Hawkins, Raleigh and the other swashbuckling seafarers. High unemployment encouraged a steady stream of volunteers to join the ranks of the queen's armies in the Low Countries, France and Ireland. Elizabethan England remained very much a man's world despite having a female monarch.

ELIZABETHAN ARMOUR

This suit of armour was made for Lord Compton. Armour in Elizabeth's reign was largely used for ceremonial occasions such as tilts. Sir Philip Sidney, however, was fatally wounded at the Battle of Zutphen because he failed to wear protective armour on his legs.

ELIZABETHAN WOMEN

'Wives are young men's mistresses, companions for middle age, and old men's nurses.'

Francis Bacon, Essays

CHOLMONDELEY LADIES
This superb early 17th-century painting is now in Tate Britain. It portrays two ladies named Cholmondeley who were born on the same day, married on the same day and gave birth on the same day.

IRONICALLY BACON MADE a late disastrous marriage to a much younger wife, yet his rather chauvinistic comment (see above) reflects the conventional male attitude towards Elizabethan women. Perceived 16th-century wisdom indicated that women were expected to marry and produce children. Ninety per cent of the adult population were married, women usually by their mid twenties, men a few years later. Any woman who was not

CELEBRATING MARRIAGE

'There was good cheer as ever was known, with all manner of musick and dancing, all the Remaining of the Day: and at night a goodly Supper; and then followed by a Masque till Midnight.' This is how John Stow described an Elizabethan wedding in London, which lasted two whole days.

married by the age of 30 was regarded with grave suspicion, sometimes even considered to be a witch. Most Elizabethan women wanted to acquire a husband for the financial security and social status of married life, conveniently ignoring the perils of childbirth.

A GAME OF CARDS
Card games were very popular with Elizabethans. The queen apparently enjoyed cards and was even rumoured to cheat in order to win.

PORTRAIT OF AN UNKNOWN LADY
Painted by Marcus Gheeraerts, this contented, heavily pregnant lady is smothered in pearls, a symbol of purity and an indication of her wealth.

after marriage a woman's entire property passed to her husband and it would have been impossible for a woman to obtain a divorce. Although Elizabethan society adopted a relaxed attitude towards male infidelities, any woman found committing adultery could expect no mercy and was likely to be completely ostracized. It may, therefore, seem surprising that foreign visitors considered that English women enjoyed far greater freedom than their Continental counterparts. English ladies were seen as immodest in their dress and behaviour, frivolous in their attitude and neglectful of their wifely duties. 'Well dressed, fond of taking it easy … commonly leaving the care of household matters to their servants,' according to Emanuel van Meteren, who was a Dutch merchant living in London during the late 16th century. The Dutch scholar Erasmus had been shocked yet secretly delighted that English ladies encouraged him to kiss them on the mouth.

Although the queen chose commitment to her duty as monarch over marriage, there is little indication that she acted as a role model for women, or did anything to help or encourage their advancement in her kingdom. Women were not permitted to enter the universities, professions or parliament, so most working women engaged in traditional female roles such as midwifery, domestic service and dressmaking – although there was a surprising number of women innkeepers!

An Elizabethan farmer's wife was expected to be able to support her husband in all aspects of life on the farm, such as animal husbandry, milking cows and making butter and cheese. She took produce to

market and kept the profits for herself. Furthermore a widow often successfully ran her late husband's business or farm. Similarly, a housewife would be responsible for every aspect of running the home: a woman's role may have been subservient, yet was essential.

A FAMILY PORTRAIT

The painting of Barbara Gamage and her six children in 1596 by Marcus Gheeraerts is now at Penshurst Place in Kent. While all the children wear skirts, the two with their mother's hands resting upon them are in fact boys.

CHILDHOOD WAS HAZARDOUS: two thirds of all babies born in Stratford-upon-Avon in the same year as Shakespeare died before reaching their first birthday, and one third of all 16th-century children failed to live more than ten years. Growing up was far from easy in Elizabethan England.

Husbands were rarely allowed to attend childbirth. The expectant mother was cared for by the midwife and her attendants, often with a crowd of female friends and well-wishers watching the baby being delivered. The proud father was then presented with his offspring by the midwife, with the time-honoured saying, 'Father, see there is your child. God give you much joy with it, or take it speedily to His bliss.'

Baptism customarily took place within three days of birth or, at the latest, by the following Sabbath. Failure by parents to baptize their child could lead to enforced baptism by the authorities, or even imprisonment. The ceremony was very similar to that of the present day, except that the godparents chose the name of the child. The arrival of a new baby always provided an excuse for great celebrations.

EDUCATING YOUNG ELIZABETHANS

The class listens intently to the teacher, their concentration undoubtedly enhanced by the proximity of the cane he is holding. This woodcut dates from the mid-16th century.

Elizabethans loved to party and festivities normally began shortly after the birth of a child, continuing until the end of the evening after the baptism, leaving the baby's head not merely wetted but positively drenched.

There was little time for play as children grew up. They were required to show adults great respect, speaking only when spoken to and at all times meekly accepting the word of their elders and betters. Parents were addressed as sir or madam at all times. Cheeky children were definitely not tolerated.

HARROW SCHOOL

This famous English public school in North London was founded with a charter from Queen Elizabeth in 1572. Lord Byron and Sir Winston Churchill later became two of the school's prominent pupils.

If the lives of Elizabethan women could be considered restricted, then those of schoolchildren were even more so. School hours were extremely long, up to 12 hours a day, six days a week; lessons by modern standards were dreadfully boring – a constant diet of Latin and Greek, punctuated by frequent beatings from sadistic masters. Only boys attended grammar school, as girls were excluded. Boys from poorer homes often had no schooling either, because they were needed to help their parents.

Famous public schools such as Harrow, Westminster and Merchant Taylors were founded during Elizabeth's reign and the number of grammar schools increased considerably. William Shakespeare went to the local grammar school in Stratford. Named King Edward VI New School, it was neither new nor founded by Elizabeth's half-brother, but dated from the early 15th century. More than 40 pupils, aged between seven and fourteen, sat in a large room above the Guildhall, which can still be seen today. Classes began at 7 a.m. in winter and an hour earlier in summer, continuing until 6 p.m. throughout the year. There were no tuition fees but pupils had to provide their own quills for writing, a knife to sharpen the quills, paper, which was very expensive, and candles in winter.

Scholarships were available after school, enabling gifted male students from poor families to enter university. It is thought that Shakespeare did not go to university because he had been taken out of school when his father ran into financial difficulties and before his education was complete.

THE ENGLISH RENAISSANCE

THE CULTURAL REVOLUTION known as the
Renaissance – the rediscovery of Greek
and Roman ideas during the 14th and
15th centuries – was slow to arrive in
England, particularly in the visual arts.
While Leonardo da Vinci, Brunelleschi
and Donatello flourished in Italy, the
nation had been engrossed in the Wars
of the Roses. These were followed by
Henry VIII's dramatic break with Rome,
which discouraged any connection with
an artistic movement that was focused
on the pope, the major sponsor of artists
such as Michelangelo and Raphael.
During the reigns of Edward and Mary
following Henry's death, England became
poorer, with no equivalent of the Medicis
to provide patronage for creative talent.
Additionally, hard-line Protestant opin-
ion associated painting and sculpture
with idolatry. Thus, as the Renaissance
swept across Continental Europe,
England was left behind.

By the mid-16th century all this began to
change through a combination of unre-
lated and unforeseen circumstances –
producing far-reaching consequences.
Roman Catholic persecution of
Protestants in the Low Countries forced a
number of gifted painters to seek artistic
asylum in Protestant England, influenc-
ing native-born artists and helping to
create a definitive English School. Henry's
dissolution of the monasteries had freed
up considerable amounts of land and

TO THE RIGHT
HONOVRABLE, HENRY
VVriothesley, Earle of Southhampton,
and Baron of Titchfield.

THE loue I dedicate to your
Lordship is without end:wher-
of this Pamphlet without beginning is but a superfluous
Moity. The warrant I haue of
your Honourable disposition,
not the worth of my vntutord
Lines makes it assured of acceptance. VVhat I haue
done is yours, what I haue to doe is yours, being
part in all I haue, deuoted yours. VVere my worth
greater, my duety would shew greater, meane time,
as it is, it is bound to your Lordship; To whom I wish
long life still lengthned with all happinesse.

Your Lordships in all duety.

William Shakespeare.

A 2

building materials, causing an explosion
in property development which greatly
benefited architecture.

Queen Elizabeth's enthusiasm for education and learning triggered a huge interest in literature, particularly poetry and
plays, and this led to professional theatre.
Similarly, the queen's love of music
assisted composers and musicians. This
warmer cultural climate encouraged the
creative talents of the painter Nicholas
Hilliard, the composer Thomas Tallis,
the poet John Donne, and playwrights
Christopher Marlowe and the greatest of
them all – William Shakespeare.

PORTRAIT OF POET
WITH HAT

*John Donne's work was not
published in his lifetime, yet he
is now regarded as one of the
nation's finest ever poets.*

ART AND ARTISTS

THE QUEEN WAS EXCEEDINGLY VAIN and enjoyed being portrayed in the best possible light. Her Privy Council also astutely realized that a flattering portrait was an excellent way of projecting the royal image to the world at large, and so art became a key element in the Elizabethan propaganda machine. The production of royal portraits became rigorously controlled and artists who were not granted the privilege of a sitting had to use 'a face pattern', a kind of stencil called a visual mechanical format issued by the Privy Council to ensure a politically correct painting – the Elizabethan version of artistic licence!

'There is no evidence that Elizabeth had much taste for painting, but she loved pictures of herself.'
Horace Walpole

ON GUARD

Sir Walter Raleigh in his prime. Queen Elizabeth appointed him to the prestigious post of Captain of the Guard, responsible for the sovereign's personal safety. However, no further honours came his way.

THE QUEEN IN MINIATURE

Queen Elizabeth painted by Nicholas Hilliard, the foremost exponent of the art of limning until his former pupil Isaac Oliver, a French Huguenot refugee, became more popular.

As the queen aged, the Privy Council encouraged painters to use 'The Mask of Youth', wherein the queen was depicted in a highly stylized manner, radiating eternal youthful beauty, a classic goddess in all her glory. Most of the best-known portraits of Elizabeth adopted this approach, including Marcus Gheereart's celebrated *Rainbow Portrait*, the famous *Procession to Blackfriars* attributed to Robert Peake and Rowland Lockey's portrait which hangs in Hardwick Hall (see page 17). In all these paintings the queen's face is identical in appearance and pose. Ironically, Protestants regarded religious portraits of the Virgin Mary as idolatrous, yet here was Elizabeth – the glowing Virgin Queen. Most Elizabethan artists fell into line: a sensible career move – English art had become state controlled in the interest of royal public relations.

As in most matters, Elizabeth was ultra-conservative in her attitude toward art: 'The queen cares not for novelties,' noted de Maisse. She disliked chiaroscuro, a relatively new approach, using light and shade to achieve dramatic highlights – a technique which Caravaggio adopted to great effect. Conservative royal taste resulted in most Elizabethan paintings appearing flat and two-dimensional, with no light and shade or linear perspective, thereby ignoring the essential ingredients of Renaissance art. Gheeraert's 'Ditchley' portrait (see page 5), the largest ever painted of the queen, was a rare example of chiaroscuro being used in a portrait of Elizabeth. English art towards the end of the 16th century was essentially neo-medieval, an outstanding example being George Gower's 'Armada' portrait (see page 71) at Woburn Abbey, a magnificent iconographic image, one of the world's most important historical pictures.

Most of these works contain complex symbolism, thus the white ermine perched incongruously on the queen's arm in George Seager's portrait at Hatfield represents purity (see page 21). Another feature was the growth of limning, portrait painting in miniature, the greatest exponent being Nicholas Hilliard, the first English-born artist to achieve international recognition. It became highly fashionable to wear a miniature of the queen to publicly demonstrate loyalty.

ELIZABETHAN LADY
George Gower gained his reputation painting fashionable ladies such as Elizabeth Sydenham, the second wife of Sir Francis Drake. The painting now hangs in Buckland Abbey in Devon, once owned by Drake. Gower's most famous work is the 'Armada' portrait of Queen Elizabeth.

Elizabeth's more cultured courtiers, including the Earl of Essex, Francis Walsingham, Robert Cecil and the Earl of Leicester, followed the queen's example and commissioned portraits of themselves or their beloved sovereign. Thus through a combination of vanity, propaganda and sycophancy, Elizabethan painting flourished – not exactly cutting edge or state of the art, yet reflecting all the glitz and glory of a vibrant age.

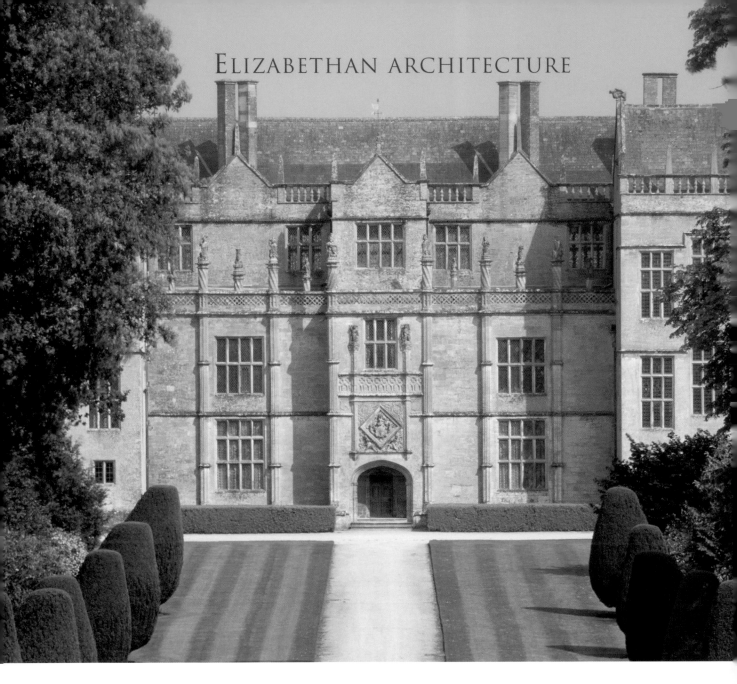

ELIZABETHAN ARCHITECTURE

ENTRY TO A GRAND HOUSE

The approach down the long drive to Montacute sets the scene for one of England's great Elizabethan homes, created in the latter years of the queen's reign by the wealthy lawyer Sir Edward Phelips.

UNLIKE HER FATHER, Henry VIII, Elizabeth displayed little enthusiasm for building; she already had more than enough royal palaces without adding to them, so she created no new ones during her lifetime nor significantly extended any existing. Likewise, the frugal queen declined to instigate any prestigious new public buildings on account of expense. Furthermore, Henry's dissolution of the monasteries had severely depleted the wealth of the Church, rendering it incapable of emulating the patronage of the pope. No new cathedrals were built in Elizabethan England, despite the religious fervour accompanying the reintroduction of the Protestant faith, because of their association with Roman Catholicism.

Establishment indifference could have proved fatal to the development of English architecture, but salvation was to appear

THE MASTER BUILDER

Three of the finest surviving Elizabethan houses, Longleat, Hardwick Hall and Wollaton Hall, were the work of Roger Smythson, the nation's first 'name architect', originally a master mason. Between the mid 16th century and his death in 1614, aged nearly 80, Smythson worked extensively throughout England and was virtually single-handedly responsible for establishing a new style of architecture, reflecting the essence of the Renaissance yet projecting the robust, self-confident exuberance of Elizabethan England. Inscribed on his monument is 'Architect and Surveyour unto the most worthy house of Wollaton and divers others of great account'.

from an entirely new source in the shape of Elizabethan entrepreneurs wishing to flaunt their new-found wealth by building huge, magnificent houses and sparing no expense. Egotists such as Sir John Thynne at Longleat and the Countess of Shrewsbury, better known as Bess of Hardwick, became the new patrons of English architecture.

A national identity was achieved by skilfully blending Renaissance principles with the High Perpendicular, the final phase of the Gothic movement, so avoiding becoming a pale imitation of stylish Continental architecture 'after the Italian modell'. The main characteristics of Elizabethan architecture were elegant symmetrical façades and the extensive use of glass, the latter being a flagrant status symbol since glass was exceedingly expensive in the 16th century. This looked impressive but had its disadvantages. 'You shall have sometimes fair houses so full of glass that one cannot tell where to be out of the sun or cold,' complained Francis Bacon. Certainly until the advent of central heating, houses such as Hardwick were bitterly cold in the winter. These buildings were tall, invariably three storeys high, as at Longleat, Burghley, Hardwick, Wollaton and Montacute, and often had flat roofs behind bulky balustrades, ideal for admiring the view or dining alfresco.

The queen appeared to believe that all property development in her kingdom was a matter for private enterprise rather than the Crown. Thus, new university colleges created during her lifetime such as Emmanuel, Magdalene and Sidney Sussex at Cambridge and Jesus College, Oxford, were all funded by private individuals, as indeed was the Royal Exchange in London, constructed in the 1560s by the wealthy financier Sir Thomas Gresham. From what appeared to be unpromising circumstances Renaissance architecture finally became established in England, albeit many years after it had in Continental Europe.

A GREAT PRODIGY HOUSE

The magnificent façade of Burghley House, one of the most prominent buildings of the Elizabethan age. Its owner, Lord Burghley, designed the house himself with the aid of a Flemish master mason.

DESIGNED TO IMPRESS

One of the corner towers at Hardwick Hall clearly shows Bess's initials and the coronet of a countess. Egotistical Elizabethans certainly believed in the maxim, 'If you've got it – flaunt it!'

43

SONG AND DANCE

THE QUEEN EXERCISED a major influence on the development of music throughout her reign, having inherited her enthusiasm from her father Henry VIII, a talented musician, reputed to have composed *Greensleeves*. Elizabeth was also an accomplished musician, being particularly proficient on the virginals, a small keyboard instrument that became increasingly popular during the 16th century. She practised every day, deriving considerable pleasure from impressing foreign dignitaries with her skilful playing.

numquam habui (In no other is my hope) is a glorious experience. Byrd, Tallis and, to a lesser extent, John Dowland collectively elevated English music from the 'hey nonny no' of folk song to a more classical plane, paving the way for Henry Purcell and Handel. Dowland was famed for his madrigals and music for solo lute, but the most famous piece written in Elizabethan England was by Doctor John Bull, organist at the Chapel Royal, who composed *God Save the Queen*, long before it became the national anthem.

FASHIONED FOR A QUEEN
This orpharian, a six-stringed instrument made in wood, was reputedly made by John Rose c.1580 for Queen Elizabeth. It is now housed in Helmington Hall in Suffolk.

'If music be the food of love, play on; Give me excess of it …'
William Shakespeare, Twelfth Night

The normally parsimonious queen employed a choir of some 50 singers at Court whose expertise also impressed visiting ambassadors. However, Elizabeth's greatest service to English music in the later 16th century was her enthusiastic patronage of William Byrd and Thomas Tallis, all the more remarkable as both were Roman Catholic. Byrd has been called the father of the English keyboard, the rich quality of his work contrasting with the more austere compositions of Thomas Tallis. Hearing a choir perform his *Spem in alium*

Dancing was a pastime that appealed hugely to Elizabethans, whether energetically cavorting around the maypole on the village green to dances with merry-sounding names like 'Lady Carew's dompe' and 'the Bishop of Chester's jig', or dancing more sedately within the sophisticated confines of Court.

ELIZABETHAN MUSICIANS

This 16th-century frieze is in the Great Chamber at Gilling Castle in Yorkshire. Music was extremely popular and, like the rock stars of today, musicians could command large sums of money to perform.

A firm favourite of the queen was the volta, where the man lifted his partner high in the air (see page 15). Equally popular was the pavane, a slow stately dance of Spanish origin, together with the galliard, danced briskly in triple time and featuring jumps termed 'capriols', from which the word capers derives.

Attention-seeking courtiers utilized dancing to get noticed by the queen – Sir Christopher Hatton is said to have caught Elizabeth's eye with his skilful interpretation of the galliard at the Inner Temple in 1561. When later created Lord Chancellor, Hatton was immediately nick-named 'the dancing chancellor'.

ON WITH THE DANCE!

Paulus Vredmann's painting depicts dancing, a pastime popular at all levels of society, be it in the Great Hall or around the village maypole.

THE DANCING QUEEN

Dancing was one of Elizabeth's passions which she continued to enjoy throughout her lifetime. The young French diplomat de Maisse wrote to King Henri IV, **'She takes great pleasure in dancing and music,** in her youth she danced very well, and composed measures and music and had played them herself and danced them. She takes such pleasure in it that when her Maids dance, she follows the cadence with her head, and foot. She rebukes them if they do not dance to her liking and without doubt she is mistress of the art, having learnt in the Italian manner to dance high.'

POETRY AND PROSE

'No spring, nor summer beauty hath such grace,
As I have seen in one autumnal face.' John Donne

SIR PHILIP SIDNEY

A miniature portrait of the gifted Elizabethan poet who wrote exquisite sonnets and the prose romance Arcadia. *He died when he was only 32 years old while fighting the Spanish army in the Netherlands.*

PROSE AND POETRY FLOURISHED in Elizabethan England; indeed it was a golden age of English poetry, featuring such poets as Sir Philip Sidney, Edmund Spenser, Michael Drayton and the inimitable John Donne. Sidney tragically died young, his reputation stemming from his prose romance *Arcadia*. When he died of a wound from the Battle of Zutphen in 1586, Sidney became the first commoner to be awarded the honour of a state funeral in St Paul's Cathedral, like Lawrence of Arabia and Sir Winston Churchill many years later.

Spenser's fame was assured by his *Faerie Queene*, a long poem which features Elizabeth in the euphoric aftermath of the defeat of the Armada. The accomplished Drayton was a close friend of Shakespeare and was with him and Ben Jonson the night before Shakespeare's death, supposedly as a result of a heavy drinking session.

Donne's verse was not published in collected form during his lifetime, yet he is now regarded as one of the nation's finest poets on account of his deft and delicate usage of language:

> 'Come live with me, and be my love,
> And we will some new pleasures prove
> Of golden sands, and crystal brooks,
> With silken lines, and silver hooks.'

Donne's father was an ironmonger and he was brought up a Roman Catholic but converted to the Protestant faith and later became Dean of St Paul's. He was notorious in his youth for riotous living and was continually poor, with a perpetually pregnant, long-suffering wife.

Elsewhere in 16th-century literary England, Richard Hakluyt's *Principal*

A UNIVERSITY LIBRARY

Sir Thomas Bodley was a wealthy career diplomat. Having retired from the queen's service in 1597, he dedicated himself to restoring the sadly rundown library at Oxford which had originally been founded in the 15th century by Humphrey, Duke of Gloucester. When it reopened in 1602 it was named the Bodleian Library. Today it continues as the university library with an international reputation amongst students and scholars alike.

Navigations, Voyages, Traffiques and Discoveries of the English Nation were evocative accounts of an age of discovery and superb early travel books. John Stow's *Annals* provided a vivid insight into Elizabethan London, where traffic congestion was already becoming a problem, Stow grumbling that, 'the world runs on wheels with many whose parents were glad to go on foot.'

William Camden's *Annals of Queen Elizabeth*, written in the reign of James I, and *Britannia* convey a detailed account of Elizabeth, her kingdom, and the important events of the age. Camden possessed a colourful turn of phrase, the fields of Bedfordshire 'smelling sweet in summer of fresh beans', while Spanish ships surged up the Channel, 'the ocean groaning under the weight of them'. He was a modest man and turned down a knighthood. Towards the end of Elizabeth's reign Francis Bacon penned his remarkable *Essays*, full of wit and wisdom, setting a scholarly seal on the literature of Elizabethan England, ushering in a lasting reputation as a literary nation.

A LEADING SCHOLAR
William Camden wrote a number of books and was commissioned by Lord Burghley to write the first biography of Queen Elizabeth towards the end of her reign.

IN THE SUMMER OF 1567 an enterprising grocer named John Brayne opened The Red Lion in Stepney, London's first-ever purpose-built playhouse for regular theatrical performances. Previously plays were acted by groups of travelling players in private houses, in the courtyards of coaching inns – anywhere suitable where authority to perform could be acquired. Without this authority actors were regarded as vagabonds by officialdom – and punished accordingly.

Some years later, Brayne went into partnership with his brother-in-law, John Burbage, in a playhouse called The Theatre, just outside the Bishopsgate entrance to the City, beyond the jurisdiction of the Puritan City Fathers who regarded playhouses as places of potential disorder, disease, and moral depravity. Subsequent theatres, such as the Curtain, were all built outside the City, the Swan, the Rose and the Globe being on the south bank of the River Thames in Southwark, an area teaming with sleazy taverns, gambling dens, brothels and every conceivable form of vice – all ironically on land owned by the Church.

Fortunately, Elizabethan actors had powerful patrons in the queen and her Privy Council. Elizabeth adored plays and her more cultured courtiers supported their own theatrical companies such as the Earl of Leicester's Men, the Lord Chamberlain's Men and the Lord Admiral's Men. These high-class minders protected the actors from virtually everything except periodic outbreaks of the plague, which closed all theatres and forced the actors to go on tour around the country.

48

A FAMOUS ACTOR

Edward Alleyn's portrait in the Victoria and Albert Museum, London. He was one of the most eminent actors of the age, starring with the Lord Admiral's Men at Philip Henslowe's Rose Theatre on Bankside. Alleyn became very rich and founded Dulwich College.

A MARLOWE MASTERPIECE

The frontispiece of one of Christopher Marlowe's greatest plays. Edward Alleyn invariably took the lead in Marlowe's plays, his powerful voice proving perfect for projecting the stirring verse.

The Tragicall History of the Life and Death of *Doctor Faustus.*

Written by *Ch. Marklin.*

LONDON,

Elizabethan theatres had roofed stages projecting into a large empty space, open to the sky and surrounded by covered galleries. Spectators paid one penny to stand around the stage and were nicknamed 'groundlings'. Another penny purchased a seat in the covered gallery. Elizabethan audiences behaved like spectators at a modern football match. They raucously cheered and jeered, drank beer and ate fruit, which they threw at the actors whenever they were unimpressed by their performance.

Theatre became the new art form of the Elizabethan age. Rising educational standards, more leisure time and increasing demand for new forms of entertainment all combined to make the theatre enormously popular. Towards the end of Elizabeth's reign it was estimated that 20,000 people a week watched the London plays – out of a total population of around 200,000! Commercial and cultural considerations combined to create show business.

Performances took place in the afternoon; there was no lighting, minimal scenery, but elaborate costumes for the actors, who were all male. A different play was produced each day, putting considerable pressures on the actor's memory but creating huge demand for writers. These included Thomas Dekker, Thomas Kyd and the 'University Wits', men such as Robert Greene and Thomas Nash who were educated at Oxford or Cambridge, frantically scribbling clever verses when not getting spectacularly drunk. The amusing but thoroughly unscrupulous Greene once boasted that he had sold the same play to two separate impresarios. Towering above them all was Christopher Marlowe. This was the cultural cauldron that young William Shakespeare encountered when he arrived in London during the late 1580s.

ALL THE WORLD'S A STAGE
This picture in the British Library shows actors performing in the late 16th century. Actors such as Edward Alleyn, William Kempe and Richard Burbage attained the fame enjoyed by film stars today.

GEORGE INN, SOUTHWARK
Now owned by the National Trust, the George Inn, near London Bridge, is a good example of the type of coaching inn where plays were performed in a galleried courtyard, prior to purpose-built theatres.

49

WILLIAM SHAKESPEARE, THE MAN

THE BIRTHPLACE

Shakespeare was born in this house in Henley Street, Stratford-upon-Avon, in late April 1564. He was baptized three days later, as was customary in an age of high infant mortality.

SHAKESPEARE'S PLAYS AND POEMS are well known throughout the world, yet the man who created them remains shrouded in mystery with many unanswered questions concerning his spectacularly successful career. Precisely what prompted him to leave Stratford-upon-Avon and go to London? Where was he during the 'lost years' between Stratford and London? How did he so quickly break into the highly competitive world of Elizabethan theatre and attract such powerful patrons as the Earls of Pembroke and Southampton? Why, at the height of his fame, did he abruptly cease writing and return to Stratford? Why is his name not on his tombstone?

Shakespeare earned a fortune from writing and became internationally famous, yet left almost no written evidence of his personal life – no letters, no diaries, no detailed records. Lack of hard fact encourages myth to fill the void. As a youth he was supposedly caught and punished for poaching deer from Charlecote, outside Stratford, yet there was no deer park there in Elizabethan times. It is claimed that he was secretly a Roman Catholic, yet there is little to support this. The erotic flavour of the early sonnets is said to indicate that he was homosexual. Most fanciful of all was James Wilmot's late 18th-century theory, that the works attributed to Shakespeare were really conceived by Francis Bacon.

Curiously, for someone who created so many star-crossed lovers and romantic love stories, there is little, apart from his guilt-ridden early sonnets, to suggest that Shakespeare enjoyed any passionate affairs. These works portray a love triangle with a poet lusting after a beautiful youth, who was having an affair with the poet's married mistress, the mysterious 'dark lady'.

LOVERS' TRYST

Anne Hathaway's cottage at Shottery, a small hamlet three miles outside Stratford. This picturesque cottage, which Anne shared with her brother, would have been a convenient place for Shakespeare to do his courting.

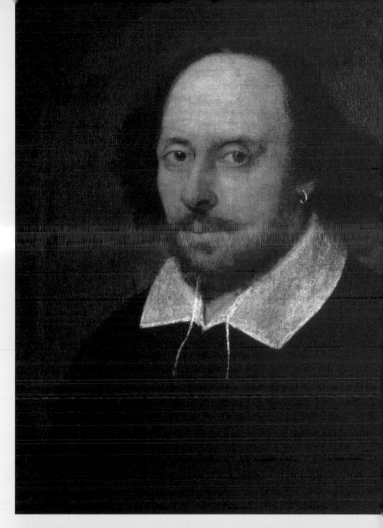

PORTRAIT OF A GENIUS

John Taylor's painting shows Shakespeare wearing a jaunty gold earring. 'He was not of an age, but for all time,' declared fellow playwright and friend Ben Jonson, after Shakespeare had died in the late spring of 1616.

A few facts are known. Pressured into marriage at an early age, after making Anne Hathaway pregnant, Shakespeare soon left the family home, first supposedly to go to Lancashire and later to London with a group of travelling players. Here he encountered the 'University Wits', sniggering intellectual snobs who looked down their literary noses at this country lad and jumped-up grammar-school boy who had the effrontery to 'out brave better pens with swelling bombast of bragging blank verse'. Shakespeare had the last laugh. The Wits' hard drinking lifestyle soon caught up with them and, by the end of Elizabeth's reign, all were dead aged less than 40, their plays dying with them. Meanwhile, the more disciplined and dedicated Shakespeare had written such enduring masterpieces as *Romeo and Juliet, A Midsummer Night's Dream, Julius Caesar* and *The Taming of the Shrew.*

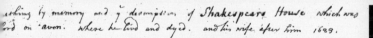

NEW PLACE

This drawing in the British Library is of a three-storey brick and timber house; it was one of the largest in Stratford and was purchased by the successful Shakespeare in 1597. He retired to New Place and later died there.

SHAKESPEARE'S RIVAL

Christopher Marlowe was the son of a cobbler and educated at Corpus Christi College, Cambridge. When Shakespeare arrived in London, Marlowe was already a successful playwright having written powerful dramas such as *The Jew of Malta* and *Tamburlaine*. The latter had a profound effect on Shakespeare, inspiring him to develop from actor to playwright. The homosexual Marlowe was a maverick, conducting a shady existence amongst London's low life, supposedly a spy, perhaps even a double agent. Aged only 29, he was murdered in mysterious circumstances in 1593, leaving the stage clear for Shakespeare.

SHAKESPEARE'S PLAYS AND POEMS

Modern-day actors duelling in Shakespeare's Romeo and Juliet, *still incredibly popular as a play and also adapted as a ballet with music by Prokofiev, and into the musical* West Side Story *by Leonard Bernstein.*

SHAKESPEARE'S STATUE

Sheemaker's marble statue of Shakespeare stands in the Front Hall of Wilton House, near Salisbury, Wiltshire, the home of the earls of Pembroke. The third earl was a patron of Shakespeare, whose company performed at Wilton.

BY CURRENT STANDARDS Shakespeare's output was prodigious, three dozen major works in barely two decades, epic historical dramas, riotous comedies, doom-laden tragedies – *Henry V, Much Ado About Nothing* and *Julius Caesar* were conceived in a single year. Yet in the context of his time, speed was essential in order to satisfy anxious impresarios, react to a rival theatre's success or exploit the latest popular trend. Shakespeare was not writing for academic approval but commercial gain. Herein was the key to his success. Whereas his university-educated rivals were engrossed with polishing their pentameters and rearranging commas, Shakespeare instinctively grasped that audiences needed to be entertained, required believable plots, situations they could identify with and recognizable characters.

Marlowe had a wonderful way with words, yet his storylines lacked coherence and continuity while Shakespeare's always maintained structure and clarity. Webster's chillingly sinister *The Duchess of Malfi* bears comparison with Shakespeare's works, but is unable to draw to a successful conclusion: Webster abruptly kills off all the main characters leaving the stage farcically littered with corpses. Thus Shakespeare remains as popular today as in the Elizabethan era, whereas Webster and Marlowe are rarely performed, Ben Jonson and John Fletcher appear dated and mannered, and other successful 16th-century playwrights, such as Thomas Kyd, have all but disappeared.

Shakespeare was fascinated by life around him, a perceptive observer of human nature which he skilfully incorporated into plays, portraying timeless themes – treachery in *Macbeth* and *Julius Caesar*, fatal mistrust in *Othello*, good overcoming evil in *Richard III*. These qualities make Shakespeare as relevant today as in his own lifetime, and he appeals to audiences across the globe.

'Be kind and courteous to this gentleman; Hop in his walks and gambol in his eyes.'

Titania in Shakespeare's A Midsummer Night's Dream

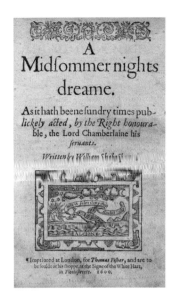

A MIDSUMMER NIGHT'S DREAM

The title page of another of Shakespeare's most successful and long-lasting plays. Originally written between 1596 and 1597, it is a lyrical tale set in Athens and features Oberon, Titania, Puck and Bottom among its many characters.

Shakespeare benefited considerably from the huge amount of foreign literature that flooded into England due to improved print technology. Thus *The Merchant of Venice, Romeo and Juliet* and *Othello* were based on Italian novellas, *Coriolanus* and *Julius Caesar* were inspired by Plutarch, and he relied on Holinshed to provide the raw material for his great historical plays such as *Richard III* and *Henry V*. Shakespeare was extremely skilful at recycling material from other sources; there was no law of copyright, and like his fellow playwrights he was prone to plagiarizing for his own purposes. Thus *Love Labours Lost* and *A Winter's Tale* derived from the 'University Wits'.

In the 1590s Shakespeare created his famous sonnets, works of intense beauty which have subsequently caused considerable scholarly angst. To whom are the poems addressed? Who is the amorous poet – is it Shakespeare himself? Who is the rival poet – perhaps it is Marlowe? Who is the enigmatic 'dark lady'? A favourite candidate is the luscious Mary Fitton, mistress of Shakespeare's patron the Earl of Pembroke. Does it really matter? Shakespeare's sonnets are exquisite, just like his plays:

'Rough winds do shake the darling buds of May,
And summer's lease hath far too short a date.'

MAN AND DOG

An engraving entitled The Constable of the Watch. *It depicts part of Act 3 of* Much Ado About Nothing, *written by Shakespeare between 1598 and 1599 when he first coined the word 'watchdog'.*

THE GLOBE THEATRE

TOWARDS THE END OF the 16th century Richard Burbage, who had inherited The Theatre in Shoreditch from his father, was unable to satisfactorily renegotiate the lease for the site on which it stood. His ingenious solution was to dismantle the building and, under the cover of darkness, transport it across the frozen River Thames, then re-erect a considerably enlarged theatre on a site close to the Rose Theatre in Southwark. The new theatre was called the Globe, its sign depicting Hercules carrying the world on his shoulders. The principal actors, amongst them Shakespeare, became partners in this venture, together with Richard Burbage, himself an accomplished actor who took the leading role in many of Shakespeare's plays. The Globe was enormous, capable of housing an audience of over 3,000, a many-sided wooden polygon, more than 30 metres (100 feet) across, with a huge platformed stage surrounded by a three-tiered gallery. The stage was nearly 2 metres (6 feet) high with no guard-rail, presenting a considerable hazard to the energetic duellists of the rival gangs in *Romeo and Juliet* – perhaps this is where the theatrical expression 'break a leg' originated!

The Globe was Elizabethan London's largest theatre and quickly became the most successful. The Lord Chamberlain's Men staged a series of Shakespeare's plays, including *As You Like It, The Merry Wives of Windsor, Twelfth Night* and *Hamlet*. All went well until 13 years after its opening, when a spark from a cannon set fire to the thatched roof during a performance of *Henry VIII*, 'consuming within less than an hour the whole house to the very ground,' according to a horrified onlooker.

A second Globe was built, similar to the first, but it too did not last. In the late 20th century the American film producer Sam Wanamaker was inspired to instigate an authentic recreation of the original Globe on a site close by. Plays are now performed there as in Shakespeare's lifetime. This imaginative venture has proved a resounding success.

A ROYAL PERFORMANCE

This Victorian painting shows Queen Elizabeth in the audience at the Globe, an unlikely occurrence, although she did attend performances at The Middle Temple, and Shakespeare's company, the Lord Chamberlain's Men, often performed at Court.

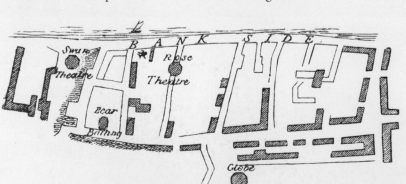

LONDON THEATRELAND

This map of Bankside shows the Elizabethan theatres clustered along the south bank of the River Thames. The present day Globe Theatre is located very close to the original site.

The original Globe Theatre

The fluttering flag signified a performance was in progress. Inscribed on the wall of the theatre was the Latin phrase 'Totus mundus agit histrionem', which translates into 'All the world's a stage', a line from As You Like It, written in 1599, the year the Globe first opened.

Premiere performance

'Friends, Romans, countrymen, lend me your ears; I come to bury Caesar, not to praise him.' The Globe Theatre opened in 1599 with the inaugural production of a new play just completed by Shakespeare – *Julius Caesar*. Thomas Platter, a visitor from Switzerland, described attending it in his *Travels Through England*: 'On the 21st of September after lunch, about 2 o' clock, I crossed the water with my party, and we saw the tragedy of the first emperor Julius Caesar acted very prettily in the house with the thatched roof, with about fifteen characters.'

Performance at the modern Globe

The recreation of the Globe, opened in 1995, has been an outstanding success with actors, audiences and critics. Here plays are produced and performed as in Shakespeare's day.

55

The conservative reaction attitude that caused England to initially disregard the Renaissance also made it slow to appreciate the significance of the discovery of the New World. By the time Elizabeth ascended the throne in 1558, the Spanish and Portuguese had already established large overseas empires, protected by powerful ocean-going fleets. In contrast, in the last year of Mary's reign, England had been driven out of Calais, its last remaining foreign possession, and the once mighty navy had become sadly neglected.

By the end of Elizabeth's reign, energetic West Countrymen such as Francis Drake, Walter Raleigh and John Hawkins, sailing from the port of Plymouth, had put England firmly on the global maritime map. Two pivotal events in the nation's history, Drake's circumnavigation of the world in 1577 and the demise of the Spanish Armada 11 years later, established England as a major sea power in the eyes of the world at large.

Queen Elizabeth's superstar sailors lived in an intensely competitive atmosphere, as each strove to gain her lucrative favours. They gathered for just one big set-piece team event – the defeat of the Armada. They were led by Lord Howard of Effingham, one of the nation's most under-rated naval commanders. This man possessed the skill to control and direct the unruly, egotistical buccaneers that were her

majesty's sea captains in one of England's greatest maritime victories, which is still celebrated annually with a special Armada Night Dinner in July, held at the officer's mess of the Royal Naval Barracks, Plymouth – appropriately named 'HMS Drake'.

THE DRAKE CUP

Buckland Abbey in South Devon contains a considerable amount of Drake memorabilia, including this beautiful cup engraved with Mercator's map of the known world in 1580. Drake probably gave this cup as a gift to a Cornish friend, Sir Anthony Rous.

A SEAFARER'S TALE

The Pre-Raphaelite picture The Boyhood of Raleigh *by Millais is in Tate Britain, London. Raleigh was fascinated by the sea from an early age, constantly seeking out fishermen and seamen to listen to their yarns.*

DRAKE'S VOYAGE AROUND THE WORLD

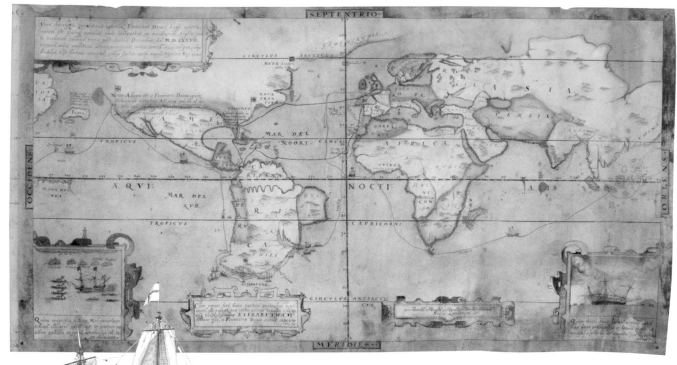

GOLDEN HIND

This model of the ship in which Drake circumnavigated the world can be found at Buckland Abbey, Devon. It was originally called The Pelican, *but renamed after the emblem on the coat of arms of Sir Christopher Hatton, one of Drake's major patrons.*

ELIZABETH HAD BEEN persuaded by the more militant members of her Privy Council to challenge Spain's maritime supremacy by commissioning a voyage deep into areas hitherto regarded by the Spanish as their own. The queen chose Drake instead of more experienced sea captains, such as John Hawkins and Martin Frobisher, shrewdly judging that he alone possessed the ambition and ability to fulfil this vital mission. Born of humble farming stock on the edge of Dartmoor, the daring, dynamic Drake was boundlessly self-confident and blessed with seemingly endless good fortune. Like many successful men he was aggressive, opportunistic and totally ruthless, with a keen eye for personal profit.

A 16TH-CENTURY CHART

This chart depicts Drake's pioneering circumnavigation of the world between 1577 and 1580. This is the earliest extant map of the voyage and is a copy of the original given by Drake to Queen Elizabeth on his return.

'This 15 day of November in the yeere of our Lord, 1577 M. Francis Drake with a fleete of five ships and barques, and to the number of 164 men, gentlemen and sailers departed from Plimmouth.'

Richard Hakluyt, Principal Navigations

HOME AGAIN

'At Mighcelmasse this yeare came Mr Fraunces Drake home to Plymouthe from the Southe Seay and mollocus and wasse round-about the world and wasse Lacke towe yeares and thre quarters and **brought home great stoore of golde and sylver in blockes**. And was afterward in the same yere for his good seruice in thatt behalf done kneighted.'

Plymouth Municipal Records, known as 'The Black Book'

Drake had first sailed offshore with his cousin John Hawkins, trading African slaves with the Spanish colonists in the Caribbean. After the pair had been attacked by the Spaniards at San Juan de Ulua, a small port in the Gulf of Mexico, Drake began plundering Spanish shipping and towns across the Caribbean, hitherto largely under Spanish control. These actions proved to be very profitable for both Drake and his queen.

Sailing in the *Golden Hind* south by south-west across the Atlantic Ocean, Drake made landfall off the coast of Brazil, and then continued towards the unexplored emptiness of the 'Great Southe Sea', where it was said lay the hitherto undiscovered 'Terra Australis Incognita', a fabled land containing treasures beyond man's wildest dreams.

Drake encountered violent storms off the tip of South America, losing contact with the other ships, never to see them again. Calmer weather finally enabled him to sail into the Pacific, then turn northwards up the west coast of South America. Drake hit the jackpot when he captured the enormous galleon *Neustra Senora de la Concepcion*, so laden with treasure that it took a week to transfer it all onto the *Golden Hind*.

Drake later landed in California claiming it for Elizabeth as 'Nova Albion'. He then turned westwards across the Pacific, narrowly avoiding disaster amongst the islands of the East Indies (now Indonesia), when the *Golden Hind* went aground on a reef. Drake's legendary luck held as a sudden storm blew his ship clear. The rest of the voyage proved uneventful, rounding the Cape of Good Hope, heading northwards once more to finally arrive in Plymouth nearly three years after setting forth. Drake was disappointed that there were no huge crowds gathered on The Hoe to witness the successful conclusion of this epic feat of seamanship: it was Sunday and everyone was in church.

SEA LIFE
Drawing of a seal made by one of the members of Drake's crew on their voyage around the world.

EXPLORATION AND COLONIZATION

EXPLORING THE
NEW WORLD

*Martin Frobisher and his men
are shown in a skirmish with
Inuits whilst searching for the
elusive North-West Passage
between Canada and the Arctic
Circle. John White's graphic
picture is in the British Museum
in London.*

16TH-CENTURY GLOBE

*Mercator, Ortelius and Frisius
were great pioneering mapmak-
ers and inventors of navigational
instruments. All were friends of
the queen's astrologer, John Dee,
who made their charts and
instruments available to English
sea captains.*

DURING THE REIGN of Henry VII, England
had missed an opportunity to spearhead
Europe's discovery of the New World.
Christopher Columbus, seeking funds for
his seminal voyage across the unknown
waters of the Atlantic Ocean, had
dispatched his brother to seek Henry's
assistance. The king agreed to help
but the brother was then captured
by pirates. By the time he escaped
Columbus had gained his funding
from Spain.

When Elizabeth came to
the throne, the Spanish
and Portuguese controlled
the richest parts of the New
World, the Portuguese also
commanding the routes to India and
the Orient. The English were left amidst
Arctic wastes, vainly trying to discover a
north-west passage from the Atlantic to
the Pacific Ocean, and exploring the east-
ern seaboard of North America, with little
prospect of finding the riches unearthed
in South America. Martin Frobisher
achieved nothing after a series of heroic
voyages trying in vain to find a sea
passage around the north of Canada.

Humphrey Gilbert perished attempting
to colonize Newfoundland. Raleigh and
Richard Grenville temporarily established
Virginia, England's first colony in North
America in 1585, only for Drake to rescue
the starving survivors the following year.

LOST AT SEA

Sir Humphrey Gilbert's largest vessel, the 120-ton *Delight*, had been wrecked off the treacherous Newfoundland coast. 'This was a heavy and grievous event, to lose at one blowe our chiefe shippe freighted with great provision ... but more was the losse of our men, which perished to the number of almost 100 soules,' lamented Edward Haye, master of the *Golden Hinde*. Gilbert rashly decided to return to England in the *Squirrel*, a vessel of barely 10 tons. It was not long before disaster struck. 'The same Monday night, about twelve of the clocke, or not long after, the Frigat being ahead of us in the *Golden Hinde*, suddenly her lights were out, whereof as it were in a moment we lost the sight, and withall our watch cried out, the general was cast away, which was too true. **For in a moment, the Frigat was devoured and swallowed up by the Sea.**'

SIR HUMPHREY GILBERT

Humphrey Gilbert was half-brother to Sir Walter Raleigh. For many years Gilbert lived at Compton Castle in Devon, which is still the family home. He was one of the most heroic, but least successful, Elizabethan sea captains.

Drake's three-year voyage around the world caused a sensation when he returned to Plymouth in 1580, yet achieved little of material benefit for the nation. The founding of the East India Company in 1600 planted the seeds of the British Empire, a term first used by John Dee, the queen's astrologer.

The idealistic Portuguese prince Henry the Navigator had been passionate about exploration, inspiring the discoveries of Bartolomeu Diaz and Vasco da Gama. Elizabeth's interest was more materialistic, the voyages of her seafarers being largely for commercial gain. If no gold or other riches transpired, the queen quickly lost interest, as Gilbert and Frobisher soon discovered. Drake was one of the few lucky enough to acquire both fame and fortune, making him an international celebrity. The Elizabethan explorers led a hazardous existence: the risk of failure was high, death a constant threat – yet the rewards could be fabulous indeed.

IN THE NEW WORLD

Painting by John White of Native Americans fishing. When Europeans landed in North America they were often helped by Native Americans, who gave them food and showed them what crops to grow.

SINGEING THE KING'S BEARD

This coat of arms is positioned above a granite fireplace in the nave of the converted abbey at Buckland in Devon.

THE BELLIGERENT FRANCIS DRAKE and his men were the queen's special forces, capable of being launched in covert operations virtually anywhere in the world, to strike with devastating force, catching the enemy completely by surprise. Drake's sudden ferocious assault on the Spanish fleet at anchor in Cadiz was precisely the audacious SAS-type raid in which he excelled: it involved speed, surprise, quick thinking and ruthless determination. Francis Bacon coined the phrase 'the singeing of the king of Spain's Beard' when he described the attack in his *Considerations Touching a War with Spain*.

This daring plan in the spring of 1587 was conceived as a pre-emptive strike on King Philip's invasion fleet before it sailed for England. The cautious queen had been persuaded to agree to this venture by the more militant members of her council – the Earl of Leicester, Sir Christopher Hatton and Sir Francis Walsingham. Drake was dispatched from Plymouth before the queen could change her mind and abort the daring enterprise.

Drake's sudden arrival in Cadiz caught the Spanish completely off guard so he was able to sail unimpeded into the outer harbour and fall upon the helpless Spanish ships at anchor. When the English finally departed, more than two dozen Spanish warships were on fire, together with a huge amount of valuable stores in warehouses on the quays. The icing on the cake came on the return voyage when a 1,000-ton Spanish merchant vessel laden with gold bullion was captured. The triumphant Drake brought it into Plymouth at the end of June 'to the great comforte of her majesty and her subjects'.

The Spanish were understandably furious. England and Spain were not at war at the time and this unprovoked attack caused considerable harm and embarrassment, making Spain the laughing stock of Europe. King Philip was determined to teach the English queen a lesson she would never forget – and capture her kingdom at the same time.

Drake was a Protestant extremist with a paranoid hatred of Catholic Spain and, like Walsingham, regarded hostilities between the two nations as a titanic ideological struggle between the forces of good and evil. He had gained his reputation privateering in the Caribbean amongst the wealthy colonies that Spain had established there. This provided rich pickings

'Thus from small things to great things.'

The inscription on Drake's drum, Buckland Abbey

DRAKE'S DRUM

This drum at Buckland Abbey is said to have belonged to Drake and was used on his last voyage in 1595. According to legend, the drum beats to summon Drake from the dead when England is in danger.

for Drake, Hawkins, Frobisher and their crews, yet their continual plundering helped to change Spain from a long-time friend into an implacable enemy, enraged that its dominance of the New World was now threatened by English upstarts.

Drake is popularly regarded as the saviour of the nation in its hour of supreme crisis, yet it could be argued that without his continual goading of Spain, for his own benefit as much as England's, all-out war might well have been avoided.

PORTRAIT OF A NATIONAL HERO
This portrait by an unknown artist was painted in the 1580s and captures Drake at the height of his fame. The picture is in the National Portrait Gallery.

COMBAT ZONE
Drake attacks the Cape Verde Islands in 1585. To the Spanish, 'El Draques' was a pirate: they called him 'master thief of the unknown world', with some justification, as England was only officially at war with Spain from 1588.

'In this yeare Sir Fraunces Drake … went here hence to the seas the thirde daie of Aprill. He arrived at Cales, where he did greatlie annoye the King of Spaine's fleete, and sett manye of fire …'
Plymouth Municipal Records, 'The Black Book'

AN ENGLISH MAN-O'-WAR

This contemporary engraving entitled The Galleon *depicts a typical Elizabethan warship with far lower topsides than its Spanish counterpart. A menacing row of cannons stretches from stem to stern.*

THE QUEEN REALIZED the importance of a strong fleet, so shrewdly appointed the veteran seafarer John Hawkins as Navy Treasurer, with the task of updating and increasing her warships. The former slave trader had become a civil servant.

'Her Majesties special and most proper defence must be her ships.'

Lord Burghley

NO COMPARISON

'The current report that strangers make of our ships amongst themselves is, that for strength, assurance, nimbleness and swiftness of sailing, there are no vessels in the world to be compared with ours.'

William Harrison, *Descriptions of England*, 1587

Using the considerable experience he had gained at sea, often in combat conditions against Spanish ships, Hawkins set about modernizing a navy that had been sadly neglected in the decade before Elizabeth came to the throne. Under his direction the traditionally high topsides were cut down, the weight was reduced and the keels deepened, in order to sail closer to the wind and become more manoeuvrable. They were, therefore, far more agile than lumbering Spanish galleons, which were ideal for long transatlantic voyages but less suited to the confined waters of the English Channel, destined to be the scene of the ultimate showdown between the two countries. When the two fleets met in the summer of 1588, nimble English warships darted with impunity amidst the cumbersome galleons of the Spanish Armada, peppering them with cannon fire.

The English warship was narrower in the beam, proportionately longer than was customary at the time and lay lower in the water: it provided an excellent floating

gun platform. This was an essential difference in the English warship as a fighting machine compared to its Spanish counterpart: English ships were constructed primarily for the use of artillery at sea, the Spanish galleons were floating castles with soldiers to board the enemy after coming alongside. Henry VIII had been fascinated by artillery and done much to develop shipboard guns mounted on wheeled gun carriages that enabled them to be fired and withdrawn for reloading far more easily than the Spanish guns, which possessed no wheels and were cumbersome to manoeuvre. Thus, the English rate of fire was far superior to that of the Spaniards, who placed little importance in gunnery, regarding it as 'an ignoble arm'. The quality of the English warships more than compensated for the larger number of galleons that were deployed against them by the Spanish.

A Spanish galleon

This engraving of a Spanish galleon, c.1580, with its towering topsides clearly demonstrates one of the fundamental differences between Spanish and English ship design.

War at sea

The English and Spanish fleets in close combat in the English Channel, supposedly watched from the shore by Queen Elizabeth. In reality she was no nearer the action than Tilbury on the Thames Estuary.

A FAMOUS VICTORY

AN AWESOME SIGHT

This picture from the Plymouth City Art Gallery and Museum shows the Armada sailing up the Channel in its familiar crescent-shaped formation, hotly pursued by the English fleet while further English ships leave Plymouth.

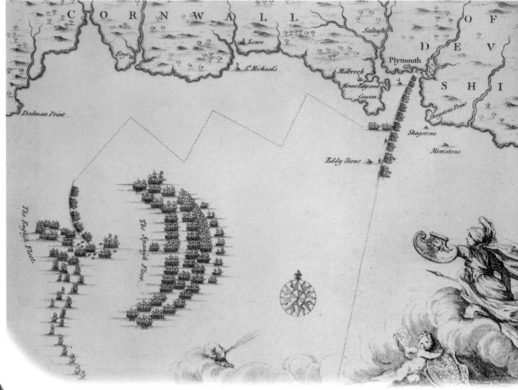

CAMPAIGN MEDAL

A commemorative medal struck to celebrate the defeat of the Spanish Armada.

THE GREATEST CRISIS OF Elizabeth I's reign came in the high summer of 1588 as the Spanish Armada surged up the English Channel to Calais, where the Duke of Parma's mighty army was to board the ships, invade England and restore Roman Catholicism. Only the English fleet could prevent this. 'If the navy had not been strong at sea what peril England would now have been in,' declared the Earl of Leicester.

The queen was not naturally warlike; nevertheless this crisis was largely of her own making. Elizabeth had allowed the hawks to gain ascendancy in her Privy Council: they encouraged her buccaneering sea captains to continually attack the Spaniards and persuaded Elizabeth to give military support to the Dutch rebels, who wanted to rid themselves of Spanish rule. The council also convinced Elizabeth to execute her Roman Catholic cousin, Mary Queen of Scots. King Philip of Spain felt that he was morally justified in attacking England – indeed it was his duty. Armed with the Pope's blessing and money, he launched his 'Enterprise of England', a crusade to instigate regime change and restore 'the true faith'.

The English were overawed by the sheer size of the Armada, mistaking troop carriers and cargo vessels for warships. Understandably cautious, they were reluctant to engage at close quarters. This was a desperate situation: if the English fleet was destroyed the nation was doomed, because most of the queen's soldiers were already deployed in the Netherlands and Ireland.

CALM IN A CRISIS

When the English learned the Armada was in the English Channel, their fleet was trapped in harbour by onshore winds and an incoming tide. Francis Drake was supposedly playing bowls on Plymouth Hoe. His airy comment, **'There is time to finish the game and beat the Spaniards after'**, could well have been true. There was little he could do – until the tide turned.

After the rival forces' initial encounter off Plymouth, there was a series of skirmishes as the Armada swaggered up the Channel towards its rendezvous with Parma, losing only a few ships en route. Sadly for the Spaniards they arrived off Calais to discover that Parma was not ready to embark his soldiers. As they waited at anchor, the English sent in fireships, forcing the Spaniards to cut their anchor cables. Prevailing winds from the south-west forced them to continue northwards, hotly pursued by the English fleet. The Spanish crews were exhausted after continual combat and their ammunition was running low.

Medina Sidonia, the Armada's inexperienced commander, made the fatal mistake of deciding to return to Spain via the north of Scotland and the treacherous west coast of Ireland. Large numbers of already seriously damaged galleons were wrecked in ferocious storms, their crews drowned or massacred as they struggled to reach the shore. When the survivors eventually reached Spain only half the Armada remained, with two thirds of the crews dead or captured. 'God blew with His winds and they were scattered,' declaimed a commemorative medal. It was indeed a famous victory – Elizabeth became the toast of Protestant Europe.

A DECISIVE ACTION

Fireships are sent in by Drake to attack the Spanish fleet at anchor off Calais. This caused the Spanish to panic, cut their anchor warps and flee north.

'All the world never saw such a force as theirs.'
Lord Howard of Effingham

A GLORIOUS DEATH

Formally a Cistercian abbey, Buckland is located in beautiful countryside in south Devon. It was successively owned by Grenville and Drake and now belongs to the National Trust and is kept as a virtual shrine to Sir Francis Drake, the legendary Elizabethan sea captain.

SIR RICHARD GRENVILLE

Painted in 1571, this fine portrait of Grenville now belongs to the National Portrait Gallery. The macho Grenville's favourite party trick was to eat wine glasses at dinner in front of his horrified guests!

ILL FORTUNE PURSUED the Grenville family like a persistently vengeful demon. Sir Richard Grenville's grandfather had been captured by Cornish rebels and imprisoned, and his father, Roger, had drowned when captain of the ill-fated *Mary Rose*, which sunk in the Solent in 1545. The queen chose Drake instead of Grenville to circumnavigate the globe, even though this was Grenville's idea. Even worse, an impoverished Grenville was forced to sell his home at Buckland Abbey to the newly enriched Drake. When the English fleet defeated the Armada in 1588, Grenville had been ordered to guard the coast of Southern Ireland – thereby missing a glorious triumph.

Grenville lusted after glory and pursued it relentlessly. Like Nelson over 200 years later, his bravery, which touched on the suicidal, led to his early death. Grenville was sailing in the *Revenge*, which had been commanded by Drake against the Armada but was now one of Lord Thomas Howard's small group of warships

cruising off the Azores. Here they encountered a far superior Spanish fleet, which was commanded by Martin de Bertendona, a survivor from the Armada, and contained 12 new galleons named after the apostles. A state of war still existed so Howard wisely decided to withdraw, but Grenville chose to stay and fight despite being hopelessly outnumbered. Fighting continued all day and throughout the night.

At dawn the next day the *Revenge* had run out of ammunition and Grenville lay dying on the deck of his badly damaged ship surrounded by Spanish galleons. The exhausted crew surrendered as Grenville's lifeblood ebbed away. 'Here die I, Richard Grenville, with a joyful and quiet mind; for I have ended my life as a true soldier ought to do, that hath fought for his country, queen, religion and honour, whereby my soul most joyfully departicth out of this body, and shall always leave behind it an everlasting fame of a valiant and true soldier.' Grenville had finally achieved the glory that he so desperately craved.

A MEMORABLE FIGHT

'In the year 1591 was that memorable fight of an English ship called the *Revenge*, under the command of Sir Richard Grenville ... This ship, for the space of fifteen hours, sate like a stag amongst hounds at bay, and was sieged and fought with, in turn, by fifteen great ships of Spain, part of a navy of fifty-five ships in all ... And amongst the fifteen ships that fought, the great *San Philippo* was one; a ship of fifteen hundred ton, prince of the twelve Sea Apostles, which was right glad when she shifted off from the *Revenge*. This brave ship the *Revenge*, being manned only with two hundred soldiers and marines, whereof eighty lay sick, yet nevertheless after a fight maintained of fifteen hours, and two ships of the enemy sunk by her side, besides many more torn and battered and great slaughter of men,' wrote Francis Bacon. Such is the stuff of legends.

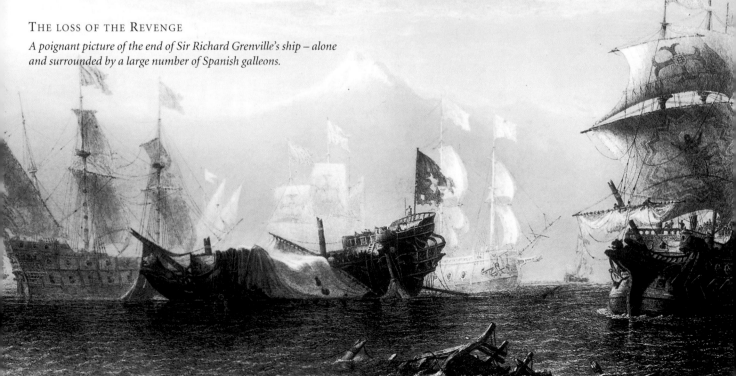

THE LOSS OF THE REVENGE
A poignant picture of the end of Sir Richard Grenville's ship – alone and surrounded by a large number of Spanish galleons.

Elizabeth, The Later Years

BY THE TIME OF THE defeat of the Spanish Armada Elizabeth had been on the English throne for almost 30 years and was 55 years old, approaching old age by the standards of the day, yet retaining generally robust good health. Inevitably the momentum of those earlier halcyon days was beginning to falter, particularly as the capable statesmen and sword-bearers, who had served her so well throughout her reign, aged with her. The death of her beloved Robert Dudley, 'sweet Robin', the same year as the victory over the Armada, represented a grievous blow to Elizabeth. Her attempt to replace Dudley with his stepson, the temperamental young Earl of Essex, proved to be a serious mistake, one which could have had potentially disastrous consequences for queen and country. This crucial error might indicate that Elizabeth's hitherto impeccable judgement of human nature was finally becoming impaired.

Nevertheless, the glory gained in so decisively defeating the Armada cast a dazzling light over Elizabeth and her kingdom, making her a living legend and conjuring up a warm glow in the sunset of her career as one of the nation's finest monarchs. It could be argued that she reigned too long and by the end of the 16th century had outlived her usefulness, yet her achievements were long lasting, benefiting both her kingdom and her subjects. Elizabeth was the last of the

THE 'ARMADA' PORTRAIT

One of the world's most important historical pictures, George Gower's portrait of the queen hangs in the Long Gallery at Woburn Abbey. The picture is full of symbolism. Elizabeth points to Virginia, England's first colony in the New World, whilst behind her the Armada sails to its doom.

FEASTING AND MASQUING

Masques, brilliantly costumed performances, often conceived by Ben Jonson together with elaborate scenery by a young Inigo Jones, became extremely popular in late Elizabethan and early Jacobean times.

great medieval monarchs – none of her successors would reign with the same supreme authority – and the last and greatest of the Tudor rulers.

THE FAERIE QUEENE

ALL ENGLAND BASKED in the euphoric aftermath of the defeat of the Spanish Armada. Both the queen and her kingdom had gained the respect and admiration of the entire civilized world, even from such implacable enemies as Pope Sixtus, who had helped to finance the Spanish Armada.

Elizabethan England became a dazzlingly vibrant place, ruled by the most glamorous monarch in the whole of Europe. Elizabeth – *Gloriana Eliza Triumphans* – was at the height of her powers, surrounded by devoted courtiers, worshipped by adoring subjects, as the great and the good flocked to Court to pay her homage.

Elizabeth was in her element, the main attraction, ever happy to be the focus of attention. Poets penned her praises; artists painted glossy pictures. George Gower's 'Armada' portrait, now hanging in Woburn Abbey, immortalizes Elizabeth for all posterity, majestic, magnificently dressed, serenely in command of all she could see.

A ROYAL PICNIC

The queen had a lifelong passion for the great outdoors. She adored country pursuits such as riding, hawking and hunting, together with picnicking in the fresh air away from the stuffiness of Court.

A ROYAL PROGRESS

Elizabeth in procession to Nonsuch Palace during a royal progress around the Surrey countryside. A progress was a public relations exercise to show herself off to her kingdom and meet and greet her citizens.

ENTERTAINING ELIZABETH

Wealthy Elizabethans were keen to entertain their queen; a royal visit was considered the height of social success, even though it could bring financial ruin if hospitality became excessive in a desire to please. Elizabeth's visit in 1560 to Basing House in Hampshire, the home of the elderly Marquess of Winchester, was a decided success. **'By my troth, if my lord were but a young man, I could find it in my heart to love him for a husband before any man in England,'** exclaimed a delighted queen. Less successful was Elizabeth's surprise visit to Berkeley Castle in Gloucestershire when the owner, Henry, the 7th Baron, was elsewhere. He returned to discover that the queen had been hunting in his deer park and all his favourite bucks had been slaughtered.

THE FAERIE QVEENE.

Difpofed into twelue books,
Fashioning
XII. Morall vertues.

LONDON
Printed for William Ponfonbie.
1590.

The Elizabethan propaganda machine deftly utilized these images to portray a fabled goddess presiding over an earthly kingdom, privileged to have her presence. The queen cleverly enhanced royal power through glittering ceremonies at Court, spectacular public pageantry, and royal progresses around the kingdom to meet and greet her subjects.

Royal progresses aside, the queen preferred the world to come to her. Surprisingly, she never travelled abroad or met any foreign monarch. Even her progresses took her no further north than Stafford or west of Bristol, and she never visited cities such as York or Plymouth.

The defeat of the Armada was the high point of Elizabeth's reign. England lacked the resources to exploit this stunning success or maintain military momentum. Further expeditions to the Azores, Cadiz and the Caribbean met with only limited success. The queen was not a belligerent person. She had defended her island kingdom in its hour of maximum danger and now preferred to rest on her laurels, to savour the joys of an epic victory.

ELIZABETHAN ESPIONAGE

SIR FRANCIS WALSINGHAM developed the nation's first secret service – an Elizabethan forerunner to MI5 and MI6 – after he was appointed Principal Secretary of State and Privy Councillor in 1573. Financing it largely out of his own pocket, he soon deployed a network of more than 100 secret agents across England and Continental Europe. Amongst them were Christopher Marlowe and perhaps even William Shakespeare. Marlowe, like Burgess, Maclean, Philby and Blunt many years later, was recruited whilst a student at Cambridge University. Marlowe could possibly have been a double agent; his mysterious, unexplained death at an East End tavern in 1593 could well indicate that he had been assassinated – anything was possible in the dangerous twilight world of international espionage.

Shakespeare is credited with originating the word 'assassination': he was obsessed with assassins and they feature in many of his major plays. Certainly the Elizabethan theatrical profession was potentially an excellent recruiting ground, the seemingly romantic role of a secret agent calculated to appeal to an actor's vivid imagination.

As the threat of war with Spain increased, government expenditure on espionage virtually trebled. It was said that there were agents located in nearly 50 places throughout Europe. This network of spies and informers certainly had its successes, unearthing the Ridolfi and Babington plots which led to Mary Queen of Scots' demise, while spies in Cadiz kept the Privy Council well informed about the preparations of the Spanish Armada.

CHRISTOPHER MARLOWE

A portrait of the great Elizabethan playwright and possible secret agent, painted in 1585 when he was a 21-year-old student at Cambridge University. Two years later he wrote Tamburlaine. *Six years later he was dead.*

for an increasingly paranoid Privy Council, as threats to queen and country loomed ever larger.

After Walsingham's death in 1590 Robert Cecil took charge and soon began to enlarge and refine the secret service. Two years after Elizabeth's reign had ended this spy network had its most spectacular success – exposing the Gunpowder Plot.

In the second half of the queen's reign, hunting down Jesuits became a major preoccupation for Walsingham's agents, as Roman Catholics were perceived as potential traitors, rather than just of a different religious persuasion. However, many spies and informers had a criminal background, more interested in easy money than loyally serving her majesty's secret service. To justify their existence, spies tended to be deliberately alarmist, grossly exaggerating potential danger and inventing plots where none existed. Thus, in some respects, the desire for increased national security merely led to greater insecurity

ANTI-JESUIT PROPAGANDA

Today this image appears somewhat jokey, but at the time John Taylor's woodcut was part of the continual and calculated attack on Roman Catholics and their faith by the Elizabethan government and its supporters.

A

Delicate, Dainty, Damnable
DIALOGVE,
Between the Devill and a Jesuite.

By *Iohn Taylor.*

LONDON,
Printed for *I. H.* for *Thomas Banks.* 1642.

'When sorrows come, they come not single spies, but in battalions.'
William Shakespeare, Hamlet

THE QUEEN IN CRISIS

TOWARDS THE END of Elizabeth's reign a new royal favourite appeared – Robert Devereux, Earl of Essex, the handsome stepson of Robert Dudley, who had died some ten years earlier. Essex was charming and courageous, yet arrogant and headstrong, reckless in his behaviour and prone to sulking when he failed to get his own way. The ageing queen seemingly saw him as a latter-day Robert Dudley, making him a Privy Councillor in 1593 and later appointing him her military commander in a disastrous campaign against Irish rebels.

THE EARL OF ESSEX

The earl's portrait, attributed to Isaac Oliver, is at Burghley House. He had inherited the title, captured the queen's affections, yet threw all these advantages away through his volatile behaviour and poor judgement.

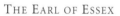

'*He is courageous and ambitious. A man of great designs, hoping to attain glory by arms.*'
de Maisse on Essex

THE IRISH PROBLEM

Ireland, England's first overseas territory, was a grave problem for Elizabeth. Supposedly ruled by the Lord Lieutenant of Ireland, in practice the English only controlled a small area around Dublin, known as the Pale, the rest of the country being held by lawless Irish chieftans prone to rebellion. Savage English reprisals caused widespread Irish misery. Matters came to a head when the Irish Earl of Tyrone caused all four Irish provinces to revolt. Essex was dispatched to crush him with a large army, but completely failed. It was left to his successor, Mountjoy, to finally defeat Tyrone although the problem was still not solved.

Elizabeth showered Essex with honours including Knight of the Garter and Master of Horse, a post she had awarded Dudley many years before. But Essex had made the mistake of antagonizing Sir Walter Raleigh and Robert Cecil. Raleigh was resentful that the younger Essex had succeeded him in the queen's affections, while the coldly calculating Cecil saw Essex as a threat to the nation, a menace which had to be removed by the most appropriate means.

Essex was in disgrace after his botched Irish campaign yet was determined to force his way back into the queen's affections and persuade her to imprison

barricaded by government troops, he panicked and fled.

Essex was soon arrested and tried for treason, one of the prosecutors being his erstwhile friend Francis Bacon, who had previously warned him of his folly. Inevitably Essex was found guilty and sentenced to death. It is unlikely that the queen would have pardoned Essex had he pleaded for mercy, but the earl was too proud anyway and Elizabeth was now well aware of the threat posed if he was allowed to live. There was no going back. On the morning of 25 February 1601, his life ended with three swift blows of the axe. Raleigh watched from the White Tower.

The queen displayed no remorse but her indulgence of this petulant Adonis represented a grave misjudgement. Essex had been popular with her subjects and, if his attempted coup had been better planned and executed, the Elizabethan era might have ended very differently. As it was, a cloud was cast over the final years of an otherwise glorious reign.

Raleigh and Cecil. He gathered around him a group of young malcontents, frustrated in their careers, contemptuous of their elders and betters, whom they regarded as totally out of touch with late 16th-century England. They included the young and impressionable Earl of Southampton, Robert Catesby, Francis Tresham and Jack Wright. Catesby later instigated the Gunpowder Plot with Tresham and Wright as fellow conspirators.

In the early spring of 1601 Essex led an armed group of his followers through the City of London towards Whitehall Palace, hoping to collect further support along the way to confront the queen. Precisely what Essex hoped to achieve by this madcap venture is impossible to fathom, for when additional supporters failed to materialize and he found the way ahead

ABANDON HOPE ALL YE WHO ENTER HERE

Traitor's Gate at the Tower of London: few who entered the Tower through this gate ever came out alive. The building, built by William the Conqueror, was a place of sadistic torture and swift execution.

TOWER GREEN, TOWER OF LONDON

This was the usual place of execution for those of high rank who had been found guilty of high treason and condemned to death. They included Anne Boleyn, Catherine Howard and the Earl of Essex.

END OF AN ERA

THE DECLINING YEARS of Elizabeth's reign saw her running out of luck as well as judgement. Her last decade experienced seven successive years of poor harvests, bringing hardship and discontent to her subjects. Her most skilful and long-serving statesmen, Leicester, Hatton, Walsingham and finally Lord Burghley, had all died, their replacements proving to be much less successful. The queen perversely refused to countenance able men such as Francis Bacon, and so too much power fell into the hands of Robert Cecil, whose main aim was to arrange his sovereign's successor. After Essex's rebellion, Cecil began to think the unthinkable – a Scottish king on the English throne. A combination of political pragmatism and self-interest motivated the wily Cecil to arrange for James VI of Scotland, son of Mary Queen of Scots, whom Elizabeth had previously executed, to become James I of both England and Scotland.

Likewise, Elizabeth's great maritime sword-bearers – Drake, Hawkins, Grenville and Frobisher – were also deceased, their successors found wanting in the art of war. So the ship of state drifted, indecisively steered, its sails poorly trimmed, its captain less capable of giving the crisp commands of earlier times.

The challenge of the Puritans had been successfully resisted; nevertheless, they had not gone away, merely been driven underground to emerge again and challenge Elizabeth's royal successors with devastating force. Similarly the querulous voice of parliament had been temporarily

BURIAL OF DRAKE

Thomas Davidson's painting at Buckland Abbey records this sombre event, when off the coast of Panama in 1596 'amidst a lament of trumpets and the thunder of the guns, the sea received her own again'. Drake was 51 years old.

However, all that lay in the future, and if, during Elizabeth's final years, the nation went into neutral, it did not slip backwards to jeopardize the successes of the glory days. The queen could rightly look back on a largely satisfactory period on the throne, during which England had been transformed from a weak, dispirited and divided nation into a major world power, whose people had a sense of pride and purpose, confident and resolute whenever danger threatened. Elizabeth had successfully met and resisted the menace of King Philip and a Spanish superpower backed by seemingly inexhaustible supplies of gold from the New World. The queen was far from being complacent: 'the beginning, though not the end, of the ruin of that king'. The phrase has a definite Churchillian ring – that was indeed her finest hour.

lulled by the queen's famous 'Golden Speech' (see page 83), but decisively reasserted itself in the following century with monarch and parliament eventually confronting each other in all-out civil war.

The Armada may well have been defeated in 1588, but conflict with Spain, although involving little largescale fighting, was still rumbling on when the queen died in 1603. Meanwhile England suffered the crippling financial burden of the large numbers of troops used to support the Dutch rebels against the Spaniards in the Netherlands, to assist the Protestant French king, and to confront Catholic insurgents in Ireland. Conceivably Elizabeth's greatest failure was her inability to provide a direct heir to maintain the Tudor dynasty, resulting in foreigners on the throne of England.

'Though God has raised me high, yet this I count the glory of my crown: that I have reigned with your loves.'

Elizabeth's 'Golden Speech', 1601

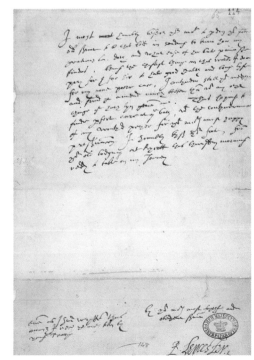

A FAREWELL LETTER

Found in a drawer alongside Elizabeth's deathbed was correspondence from the Earl of Leicester, simply marked by the queen in her own handwriting, 'his last letter'. This historic document is now in the National Archives at Kew.

WINNERS AND LOSERS

ELIZABETHAN ENGLAND was a nation full of ambition and enterprise, presenting a tantalizing prospect of fame and fortune. Competition was intense – only the most talented, dedicated and industrious would succeed; inevitably some would fare better than others, yet others would fail completely. Luck could play a crucial part: 'Some men are born great, some achieve greatness, and some have greatness thrust upon them,' wrote William Shakespeare in *Twelfth Night*.

Success in the competitive environment of Elizabethan England usually came through a desire to succeed, ruthless determination and perhaps a touch of good fortune. It was an era when a changing economic climate, coupled with a shift in social attitudes, enabled people from relatively modest backgrounds to prosper. Education was becoming more widely available and it was possible for a person of humble origin to enter university, and thereafter thrive in the variety of professions that expanded or emerged during the second half of the 16th century.

Appearance was all important: it was highly desirable to be handsome and impeccably attired in the latest fashionable outfit, particularly in the competitive crucible of Court, where patronage was a deciding factor amidst the growing climate of greed and corruption in the latter part of the period.

Certain categories of the population found it impossible to succeed. These included the majority of the poor and the English Catholics: the former were helpless victims of economic circumstances, the latter subject to extreme religious bias. This was the harsh, increasingly materialistic world of Elizabethan England – joy, wealth and prestige for the winners, for the losers, only despair and sometimes violent death.

OVER-HYPED HERO

Although history portrays Sir Walter Raleigh as a charismatic figure, in reality he achieved little of significance and his life ended with his head on the block at the Tower of London in 1618.

HOME FOR OLD SOLDIERS

The Earl of Leicester acquired these medieval premises in Warwick as a home for his pensioner soldiers and their wives. The Lord Leycester Hospital is one example of a wealthy man helping the poor and needy in a practical way.

THE TOWER OF LONDON

By Tudor times the Tower had become mainly a prison for important political prisoners. Here they could be incarcerated for many years or suffer under torturers, such as the psychopathic Richard Topcliffe.

81

Mr Speaker, Sir!

PARLIAMENT BEGAN TO FLEX its political muscles during the Elizabethan age and establish itself as a powerful voice, jealously guarding its fundamental right to freedom of speech. The queen was always careful to maintain good relations with parliament and never confronted or antagonized it, yet she failed to fully appreciate the significance of its growing powers and so did not foster a new, lasting relationship between Crown and parliament. This failure was to prove detrimental to her Stuart successors.

THE PARLIAMENTARY PROCEDURES

The frontispiece to an account of Queen Elizabeth's parliament between 23 November 1584 and 24 March 1585 – an Elizabethan forerunner to Hansard.

THE QUEEN'S SPEECH

Robert Glover's picture in the Folger Shakespeare Library in Washington DC depicts Elizabeth addressing parliament at Westminster. The queen placed great importance on parliament, with Robert Cecil and Christopher Hatton being her main representatives.

There were no official political parties in Elizabethan times: these only developed many years later, along with cabinet ministers and a Prime Minister. In the 16th century the nation continued to be governed by the monarch and the Privy Council. Parliament met less frequently than today and for shorter periods; it did not sit in the summer because of the risk of plague. Summoning or dismissing parliament was entirely the prerogative of the monarch.

Towards the end of the 16th century the Speaker of the House of Commons was Sir Edward Phelips, who created Montacute, that glorious Elizabethan house in Somerset. Phelips, a foremost lawyer of the day, was destined to play a leading role in the prosecution of Guy Fawkes. The House of Commons was subjected to progressively stronger Puritan influence – zealous reformers, pursuing a radical agenda. Their loudest voice was that of Peter Wentworth, who was only silenced when sent to the Tower of London in 1593 for unwisely agitating outside the debating chamber, where he

could no longer claim parliamentary privilege, for the queen to name her successor, a subject about which she was particularly sensitive. Wentworth remained in prison until his death four years later.

An indication of parliament's growing strength came in 1601 when it successfully persuaded the queen to abolish the iniquitous monopolies, which she had originated to enhance the pockets of her favourite courtiers. Monopolies granted sole rights to manufacture and distribute products such as wine or salt, an excellent way for the queen to enrich courtiers at no actual cost to herself. Nevertheless, the resultant high prices made monopolies massively unpopular across the nation. Elizabeth's subsequent eloquent address to a parliamentary delegation at Whitehall Palace in 1601 became known as her 'Golden Speech'. Her honeyed words on that occasion were akin to soothing a fractious child – effective and comforting. However, just two years earlier a child had been born in East Anglia who would lead a parliamentary army against the monarchy. His name was Oliver Cromwell.

SIR EDWARD PHELIPS
The Speaker of the House of Commons in the latter years of Elizabeth's reign, Sir Edward was a skilful lawyer who later played an important role in the prosecution of the Gunpowder Plotters.

POVERTY AND AFFLUENCE

'Well, whiles I am a beggar, I will rail,
And say there is no sin, but to be rich;
And, being rich, my virtue then shall be,
To say there is no vice but beggary.'

William Shakespeare, King John

SIR THOMAS GRESHAM

An extremely wealthy merchant and skilful financier during Elizabeth's reign, Sir Thomas was the queen's chief financial advisor and Keeper of the Privy Purse. He also founded the Royal Exchange.

RAPIDLY RISING INFLATION was a constant feature of the 16th century, seriously affecting all those who were on fixed wages, did not own their own land, or needed to purchase basic commodities, which were constantly rising in price. The cost of food and other essential goods required by an average working-class family increased five times during the Tudor era, causing widespread hardship. The continual closure of common land and a series of poor harvests compounded the problem.

Poverty further increased as a considerable number of disabled soldiers and sailors, injured in the continuous war against Spain, returned to England with little prospect of gaining employment.

AN UNCHARITABLE ACT

Stephen Bateman's mid-16th century woodcut pictures a wealthy, opulently dressed man spurning a beggar clad in rags. Growing poverty was one of the major problems of the Elizabethan age.

84

The authorities became alarmed about the rising number of poor across the nation, not out of any charitable concern, but because they feared widespread lawlessness as gangs of the unemployed roamed the countryside and beggars became a serious problem. In an attempt to rectify this critical situation, parliament passed the Poor Law Act in 1598, requiring each parish to care for its beggars and each town to provide a poorhouse paid for by local taxation.

MAUNDY CEREMONY

Lavinia Teerlink's miniature shows an Elizabethan Maundy ceremony when the monarch publicly distributed money to the poor. This ritual ceremony still exists in a modified form and traditionally takes place on the Thursday before Easter.

Conversely the middle classes prospered greatly. Merchants profited as trade expanded, particularly with the New World and the Orient, and a wide range of new luxury goods became available, increasing demand from a more sophisticated and affluent public. Farmers benefited from rising land prices and a fast-growing urban population totally reliant on purchasing food rather than producing it themselves.

❧

Nowhere was the contrast between rich and poor more evident than in their respective homes. The rich lived in substantial houses, usually built of stone or brick, a material that was becoming increasingly popular and widely available. Windows contained glass, expensive but highly desirable to the status-conscious Elizabethans. Tall chimneys ensured that smoke-filled rooms were a thing of the past. These rooms featured elaborately decorated plasterwork or were panelled in wood, which was brightly painted rather than polished. Floors were invariably tiled or covered in rushes on the ground floor, with polished wooden planking upstairs. Substantial furniture – usually made out of oak and beautifully carved – and tapestries enhanced the rooms.

❧

In contrast, poorer homes had improved little since the Middle Ages. They were constructed in wattle and daub with thatched roofs, providing a fertile breeding ground for insects, which caused discomfort and disease. Windows were shuttered or simply covered with sacking because glass was unaffordable. The entire family shared the same bed and a primitive toilet. In short, the rich man's house indicated his status, the poor man's abode merely provided a roof over his head.

❧

Nevertheless, Elizabethan England was a land of opportunity: with ambition, hard work and a modicum of good fortune it was perfectly possible to progress up the social scale, as proved by Sir Francis Drake and Bess of Hardwick.

PURITANS IN ASCENDANCY, CATHOLICS UNDER THREAT

'There is only one Jesus Christ; the rest is a dispute over trifles.'

Queen Elizabeth I

THE QUEEN'S LOFTY VIEW of religion expressed to the French envoy de Maisse in 1597 was not shared by the Puritans, who felt that Elizabeth's reform of the Church in England had not progressed nearly far enough. The Puritans wanted to abolish the bishops, greatly simplify clerical apparel, further reduce the interior decoration of churches and severely modify the church service. The more their hard-line views were rejected, the more they agitated and the greater their numbers grew. Often better educated than bumbling Protestant parsons, the Puritans could usually outwit them in theological debate. Puritans felt superior in thought, word and deed, morally correct and spiritually pure. Protestant theologians such as Richard Hooker in his masterly *Laws of Ecclesiastical Polity* temporarily held back this rising tide of religious extremism, only to create the ticking time bomb that exploded in the reign of Charles I. Elizabeth's tendency to procrastinate in the hope that trouble would disappear of its own accord was destined to store up severe difficulties for the Stuarts in the years to come.

PORTRAIT OF A MARTYR

Edmund Campion was the best known of the many Jesuits who were hideously tortured and put to death; paranoid hatred of Roman Catholics grew as relations with Catholic Spain reached crisis point.

A NOBLE MARTYR

Nearly 200 Roman Catholics were executed during Elizabeth's reign, the majority being priests. Amongst their number was Father Edmund Campion, perhaps the noblest of all the Catholic martyrs – scholarly and selfless, completely dedicated to his faith and its followers. Campion had studied at St John's College, Oxford, where he had made a speech of welcome to the queen when she visited the university in 1566, greatly impressing Elizabeth with his oratory. Campion then became an Anglican deacon but converted to Catholicism in 1571, later becoming a Jesuit priest in Rome. He secretly returned to England in 1580 and courageously travelled around the country conducting secret masses, preaching and hearing confessions. In the summer of 1581 he was betrayed, taken to the Tower of London and tortured. Campion graciously declined the queen's offer of a pardon providing he returned to the Protestant faith. He was hanged, drawn and quartered at Tyburn and later created a saint.

CHASTISING A CAT

Those of a less fanatical religious persuasion poked fun at religious extremism. Here a Puritan housewife is lampooned for whipping her cat for catching mice on the Sabbath.

As the religious pendulum swung towards the Puritans it moved away from the traditional English Roman Catholics, who became progressively more persecuted during Elizabeth's reign, then totally despised and demonized following the Gunpowder Plot two years after her death. It has taken several centuries for these prejudices to subside across the nation – and even now some bigotry still persists.

Certainly the greatest losers in religious terms during this period were the Roman Catholics. It was a tribute to their steadfast beliefs that so many maintained their faith in the face of such adversity, whilst continuing to be loyal to the Crown despite harsh and unjust treatment. By the second half of Elizabeth's reign politics and religion had become hopelessly intertwined and English Roman Catholics were in the invidious position of being perceived as enemies of the state in their own country – an unenviable position and much to their detriment.

A CATHOLIC SAFE HOUSE

Baddesley Clinton in Warwickshire became 'a very safe refuge' for Catholics. Leading Jesuits, such as Robert Southwell and Father Garnet, hid here. The latter stood waist deep in icy water for many hours in 1596 to avoid capture.

87

FRANCIS BACON – UNREWARDED GENIUS

LAWYER, POLITICIAN, PHILOSOPHER, scientist and essayist, the multi-talented Francis Bacon was the archetypal Renaissance man. The queen used him as her special advisor, listened to his words of wisdom, took his advice, yet gave little in return. Bacon acquired no important position or honour throughout her reign, in spite of being continually recommended for high office by the Earl of Essex, the royal favourite of the time. Friendship with the volatile earl could well have hindered rather than helped the ambitious Bacon, as Essex had made enemies of the all-powerful Lord Burghley and his talented son, Robert Cecil. Furthermore, Bacon, like his brother Anthony, was homosexual, something which would definitely not appeal to the ultra-orthodox queen. Eventually Bacon turned against Essex and was part of the prosecution in the earl's trial for treason in 1601, justifying these actions in his *Apology, Certain Imputations Concerning the Late Earle of Essex*, written the year the queen died.

THE INNS OF COURT
The gateway to Lincoln's Inn. Clever young Elizabethans, such as Hatton, Raleigh, Bacon, Sidney and Donne, learned law at one of the four Inns of Court – Gray's Inn, Lincoln's Inn, the Middle and Inner Temples – all still located between Temple Bar and the Thames.

SIR FRANCIS BACON
Following his release from the Tower, Bacon devoted himself to study. He died a bizarre death in 1626, after catching a fatal chill whilst conducting a scientific experiment freezing chickens.

Bacon was the younger son of the portly Sir Nicholas Bacon, appointed to Elizabeth's first Privy Council in 1558, brother-in-law of William Cecil, later Lord Burghley. At the age of 12, Francis entered Trinity College, Cambridge, where a marble bust of him can now be found in the Wren Library, alongside other distinguished Trinity alumni, including Sir Isaac Newton and Alfred, Lord Tennyson. Bacon and Essex first met at Trinity. Bacon then furthered his law studies at Gray's Inn, London, before entering the queen's service both in a legal capacity and as political advisor. His burning desire to gain wealth and prestige remained unfulfilled, although Bacon was desperate for both: 'money is like muck, not good except it be spread,' he wrote in his superb *Essays*, first published in 1597. They were full of acerbic one-liners, such as 'the French are wiser than they seem, the Spaniards seem wiser than they are'.

It was not until Elizabeth's reign was over and James I had become king that Bacon was finally rewarded and his legal expertise recognized. He became successively Attorney General and Lord Chancellor, knighted on the accession of James in 1603, then Baron Verulam and finally Viscount St Albans. Then disaster struck. Bacon was found guilty of taking bribes, thrown into the Tower and thoroughly disgraced. Perhaps Elizabeth's reservations about him had been justified all along.

'If parts allure thee, think how Bacon shined,
the wisest, brightest, meanest of mankind.'

Alexander Pope, Essays on Man

RALEIGH'S CELL IN THE TOWER
Raleigh was imprisoned in the Bloody Tower by James I for conspiring to put Arbella Stuart on the throne following Elizabeth's death. Here he wrote his celebrated History of the World.

THE PRICE OF FAILURE

Raleigh was another under-achiever in Elizabethan times – soldier, sailor and explorer, promising much yet producing little. Charming and good looking, Elizabeth found Raleigh entertaining but unsuitable for her Privy Council or any other key post. James I was even less impressed, letting Raleigh out of the Tower of London on condition that he find the gold of El Dorado. When he predictably failed, the king had him executed. Asked which way he would like to lay his head on the block, Raleigh – urbane unto death – replied, **'So the heart be right, it is no matter which way the head lies.'**

SUCCESS AGAINST THE ODDS

'Little Cecil trips up and down; he ruleth both Court and Crown.'   *A contemporary ditty*

ROBERT CECIL PROSPERED during Elizabeth's reign – and did even better under James I. He had the advantage of being the son of Lord Burghley, the queen's most trusted and long-serving minister, yet he suffered a number of handicaps. Cecil was barely 1.5 metres (5 feet) tall with a rather large head. He had apparently been dropped by his nursemaid as a baby, an accident that left him with a curved spine and the appearance of a hunchback, aligning him with the Shakespearean image of Richard III, much reviled in Elizabethan England.

Cecil's enemies made much of his deformities, causing him considerable resentment as he was extremely sensitive about his appearance. The queen thoughtlessly nicknamed him 'my pigmy', which upset him even more. Cecil was a relative midget amongst the macho, good-looking members of the Court, who had little liking for him. 'The world is not apt to speak well behind one's back,' he once sadly remarked to a fellow courtier. The lofty Earl of Essex disliked him intensely, literally looking down his aristocratic nose at Cecil, whom he regarded as a loathsome, irritating upstart. In turn, Cecil saw Essex as pretentious, unduly privileged and over-promoted.

Robert Cecil was a workaholic with a first-class brain. He may have been short in stature but intellectually towered head and shoulders above the other members of the Privy Council, which he had joined in 1591 at the age of 28. The coolly

HATFIELD HOUSE

James I gave Hatfield to Robert Cecil in exchange for Lord Burghley's former home in Hertfordshire. Cecil completely rebuilt the Tudor house to create the masterpiece we see today; it contains many documents relating to the Elizabethan and Jacobean eras.

SIR ROBERT CECIL

A portrait of the younger son of Lord Burghley as painted by John de Critz. Cecil's star rose under Queen Elizabeth and soared further under a grateful King James, who made him Earl of Salisbury.

calculating Cecil was more than a match for the impetuous Earl of Essex, their frequent clashes akin to the explosive encounters between matador and charging bull. After Essex was executed for treason in 1601, Cecil ruled supreme until the queen's death two years later.

Cecil was astute and extremely focused; he was a superb administrator, keen, conscientious, invariably to be seen 'with his hands full of papers and his head full of matter'. He regularly attended parliament where he proved an articulate speaker, succinct, with a quick grasp of his subject, logical in thought, persuasive in word. The queen trusted him implicitly – and knighted him in 1590.

James I, who was well aware that it was largely due to Cecil that he had acquired the English throne, quickly created him Earl of Salisbury and gave him Hatfield House, which Cecil proceeded to rebuild as the magnificent home where the Salisbury family still live today. The Salisburys' link with parliament has lasted many centuries. The Marquess of Salisbury was Prime Minister three times during the second half of the 19th century, and Viscount Cranborne, heir of the present Marquess, has been Conservative Leader of the House of Lords.

Robert Cecil only served Elizabeth in her latter years so was not overawed by her youthful vitality and beauty, but objectively impressed by her achievements: 'our blessed queen was more than a man, and in troth sometimes less than a woman' was the precise, penetrating verdict from this highly successful Elizabethan.

ENDING THE WAR

When James became king, his government quickly ended the long-running war with Spain. Cecil, on the extreme right of the picture, took part in the peace negotiations at Somerset House, London, which began in 1604.

The Chariott drawne by foure Horses vppon which charet stood the Coffin couered with purple Veluett and vppon that the representation. The Canapy borne by six Knights.

footemen.

THE QUEEN'S CORTEGE

This painting in the British Library illustrates Elizabeth's funeral procession, held at the end of April 1603, a month after her death. Her coffin was drawn by four horses 'trapped with black velvet beset with the arms of England and France'.

THE FIRST STUART KING OF ENGLAND

When the Scottish King James also acquired the English throne, he wanted to combine both kingdoms to form Great Britain, a vision which was thwarted by the English parliament.

JAMES VI OF SCOTLAND took the ultimate prize – the throne of England. He attained the Crown almost by default as Elizabeth had left no direct heir and no other claimant was likely to meet with the nation's approval. Robert Cecil, however, was determined that James should succeed. Thus a Scotsman became king of England. The Scottish nation, which had suffered so grievously from invading English armies, had gained the kingdom from the 'auld enemy', without a shot being fired.

At first James was well received – at least he was not Roman Catholic. He was the first male monarch for more than half a century and the nation was ready for a change. Large numbers of English nobility eagerly galloped northwards to accompany him on his triumphant journey to London to collect the Crown. James was euphoric: he came from a poor country that was difficult to control, and now he had the riches of England within his grasp and its military might to protect him. This had been his dream and the reason he had made only a token protest when Elizabeth had executed his mother, Mary Queen of Scots.

In marked contrast to Elizabeth, James lacked stature, good looks and, above all, charisma. When he dined, he drank excessively and had a disconcerting habit of dribbling. Where Elizabeth had been frugal in her expenditure, James was excessively extravagant. Under his influence the Court became dissolute and decadent. James was intelligent but lazy; the French king derided him as 'the wisest

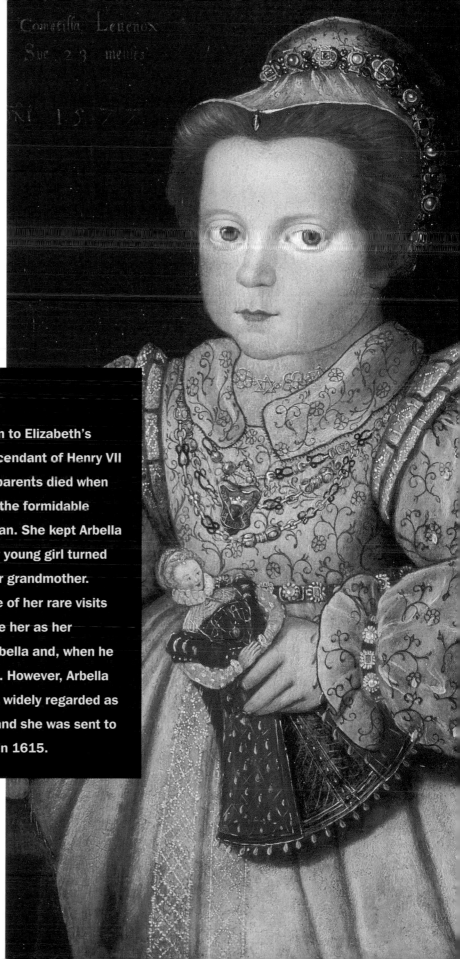

fool in Christendom'. He considered himself an intellectual and was fond of lecturing people, be they Roman Catholics, Puritans or parliament. The Catholics attempted to assassinate him with gunpowder, while the Puritans and parliament united against him.

To his credit, the new king, aided by Robert Cecil, speedily brought the long-running war with Spain to an end and his greatest act was to organize a new version of the Bible. The resultant *King James Authorized Version of the Bible*, published in 1611, was an immediate and long-lasting success.

A SAD STORY

Amongst those with a legitimate claim to Elizabeth's throne was Arbella Stuart, also a descendant of Henry VII and, unlike James, English. Both her parents died when she was young and her grandmother, the formidable Bess of Hardwick, became her guardian. She kept Arbella under strict supervision and the lively young girl turned into a neurotic spinster who hated her grandmother. Arbella had irritated the queen on one of her rare visits to court so Elizabeth declined to name her as her successor. James was attracted to Arbella and, when he became king, he brought her to Court. However, Arbella unwisely married the Earl of Hertford, widely regarded as a dangerous claimant to the throne, and she was sent to the Tower of London, where she died in 1615.

A CLAIMANT TO THE THRONE

A portrait of Arbella Stuart as a young girl, now in the Drawing Room at Hardwick Hall. As a descendant of Henry VII she had a legitimate claim to the throne, which was supported by Raleigh. Both she and Raleigh ended up in the Tower of London.

ELIZABETHAN EPILOGUE

SEAL BURSE OF ELIZABETH I

The seal burse (purse) was used to contain the Great Seal, carried in procession before the Lord Chancellor and the Keeper of the Seal. This seal was attached to all major documents of state. The burse carries the letters ER (Elizabeth Regina) and the royal coat of arms.

ANATOMY CLASS

An illustration from The Elizabethan Anatomical Tables *by John Banister (1540–1610) showing Banister lecturing attentive medical students on anatomy with the aid of a corpse and a skeleton. Such lectures were revolutionary at the time and led to the traditional view of anatomy, unchanged since* AD 175, *being challenged.*

ELIZABETH'S REIGN WAS a glorious epoch in England's history. In less than half a century the nation had risen from a position of poverty and acute peril to become a prosperous, major maritime power, respected throughout all Europe. The Renaissance had finally come to England, creating a lasting reputation as a literary nation. Protestantism had replaced Roman Catholicism as the nation's religion and the Anglican Church was permanently established. Parliament had begun the long journey towards establishing a democratic kingdom.

A MUCH-LOVED MONARCH

'When they beheld her statue lying upon the coffin, there was such **a general sighing, groaning and weeping as the like hath not been seen** or known in the memory of man, neither doth any history mention any people, time or state to make like lamentation for the death of their sovereign.' So wrote John Stow, an eyewitness at Queen Elizabeth I's funeral.

It is easy to take an unduly romantic view of Elizabethan England and the queen died leaving a significant amount of unfinished business. The war with Spain had not been won. Tensions between the monarchy, parliament and the Puritans were soon to confront the Stuart succession. The growing problem of poverty amongst the underclass was unresolved. No permanent colonies had been established abroad. Nevertheless, the queen's glittering reputation survives intact 400 years later, and the exploits of Elizabethan England continue to inspire, while Elizabeth, Drake and Shakespeare remain three of the greatest figures the nation has produced.

'This blessed plot, this earth, this realm, this England ...'
William Shakespeare, Richard II

INDEX